KADASHAN
SPEAKS

THE LAW OF NATURE AND NATURE'S GOD

VOLUME 2

OUR LIVES, OUR LIBERTIES,
OUR PURSUIT OF HAPPINESS

KADASHAN

Copyright © 2019 by Kadashan.

ISBN Softcover   978-1-949723-69-4

All rights reserved. No part of this book may be reproduced or transmitted in any form or by any means, electronic or mechanical, including photocopying, recording, or by any information storage and retrieval system without express written permission from the author, except in the case of brief quotations embodied in critical reviews and certain other non-commercial uses permitted by copyright law.

Printed in the United States of America.

P.O. box 75 Yakutat, Alaska 99689
Email: bert.adams@hughesnet.net
Website: http://www.kadashan.simplesite.net

To order additional copies of this book, contact:
Bookwhip
1-855-339-3589
https://www.bookwhip.com

This work is dedicated to the aboriginal Americans, and to the young people of America. These future patriots will have to bear the burden of bringing traditional Native American values and early American standards together once again.

CONTENTS

Introduction ix
Prologue xiii

PART ONE

Themes from Self Governance 1
Early America and the Natural Law 2
Native American Influence... 5
The Indian Reorganization Act 9
Non-BIA Programs 14
USDA (Forest Service) Demonstration Project 16
The Declaration of Independence and the U.S. Constitution
   limits Government 18
The Power to Tax 22
Who Should Own Land? 24
The Concept of State's Rights 26
Altering or Abolishing Governments 28
Our Problems are Universal Problems 32

PART TWO

The Law of Nature 33
The Law of Nature and Nature's God 34
The Spectrum of the Constitutional Eagle 38
U.S. Forest Service Sets the Pace 45

Many Solutions Found Within Our Constitution 51
Are we a Democracy or a Republic?...57
Improper Role of Government..63
Ten Cents on the Dollar..67
Absolute Power to Tax Should be a State Right 70
Let's Reflect Upon Our Taxing History 73
The Commerce Clause..76
History Offers Lesson on Home Site Program..................................79
Intent is the Key to Finding Truth 83
Indian Self-Governance..86
We Need Laws Based on Common Sense...90
We Need to Think Like the Founders..94
Where does goodness come from? 97
America Stands for Goodness...100
Combating Dependency, A Challenge for Native Communities....104
Each Tribe Must Carry Self-Governance Forward.........................108

PART THREE

The Alaska Native Brotherhood 111
One of the First..112
ANB Champions for Native Rights..116
Alaska Native Brotherhood and the Indian Reorganization Act.....121
Testimony before the Alaska Natives Commission 125
Ansca and ahe Free Enterprise System 132
Our Greatness Is Measured in Proportion to Our Goodness 135
Three Tlingits and a Genie 140
Home, the Center of All Living...144
Back to the Basics—Our Rights...149
Back to the Basics—Our Rights...153
Sometimes We Need to Go Back to Move Forward...................... 157

Management of Resources or Management of People 160
Religion in America..164
Peace and Prosperity Requires Freedom, Based on Natural Law 167
There Ought to be a Law 171

PART FOUR

Reclaiming our Heritage 173
Ramifications of First and Second-Rate People............................ 174
A New Kind of Common Sense 177
Government for the Iraqis, Of the Iraqis, By the Iraqis 180
The Spirit in Sit.. 183
Things Don't Happen by Chance... 186
A born-again what? 189
Is God on Our Side Anymore? 192
Socialism.. 195
The Impact of Socialism in the United States............................. 199
Reconciliation—Is it Constitutional?..203
A Political Isolationist...207
Someone Is Fooling with the Soul of America 211
Something Very Refreshing... 214

Epilogue 219
Bibliography 227

I have over 78 highlighted points throughout this book that I can go back to and reference when I need direction or answers to questions. I really enjoyed this book as it brought me back to the basics of what made our country great. Our founding fathers understood the importance of small government and a strong democratic society. I believe Kadashan's prescient book really should be shared with everybody. Especially in today's political climate, it could really help put our lives in perspective with respect to personal happiness and political ideology.

Sincerely,

Garrett A. S. James
Regional Sales Manager - Los Angeles, San Diego & Las Vegas
Evolution Power Tools

INTRODUCTION

I began writing for the Juneau Empire, the capital city of Alaska's newspaper because I became very much concerned about the way our governments were drifting from the fundamental principles the Founding Fathers of this great nation had created for us. In addition, I was concerned about the plight of Native American state of affairs as well. Even though the paper, in my opinion, is somewhat liberal the Managing Editor at that time thought I had something to offer about Native American politics—especially since I was Alaska Native. I had studied the U.S. Constitution when I was enrolled at Brigham Young University and as the Tribal President of the Yakutat Tlingit Tribe I was heavily involved in Alaska Native politics from 1993-2006.[1] In my writings, I emphasized that "Native Americans," and all Americans for that matter, should be concerned with modern day political issues. When we see the ways, our federal government is leading us today all true blooded Americans should be gravely concerned about the future of our beloved country—both Native and Non-Native. After all we are Americans and live under the banner of the U.S. Constitution—the very instrument that was designed to protect us from the injustices of government. These commentaries arose from my writings in a monthly column called Kadashan's Corner that I wrote for the Empire, The Tundra Times, a website called Free of State and other periodicals

---

[1] See U.S. Forest Service Sets the Pace to learn how I got involved in tribal politics.

When I began writing my column, I asked three elders—men of whom I held in high esteem—if it would be proper to use my Tlingit name, Kadashan, as my pen name. I was somewhat amazed at their response because they each gave me the same advice. They agreed it would be appropriate so long as I did not use my editorial muscle to injure the people I write about. I realized that this would be an enormous challenge because mainstream journalism these days is focused mostly on negative commentaries, so they can sell their newspapers or to increase their television ratings; although I had good reason to become a *muck rucker* in the Native American environment, especially as an Alaskan Native, I pledged that I would honor their advice. These individuals knew about my great grandfather, of whom I was named after, and they said that I should not tarnish his name or good works. [2] Admittedly there were many times when I've had to "bite my tongue" for the sake of keeping my great grandfather, and my Tlingit heritage, free from public disgrace. Following their advice has made me a better person as I tried to stick to fundamental principles that are based on the Natural Law and God's Laws. 1

There are two strong messages I hope readers find emerge in this work. Because I am deeply rooted in my Tlingit culture, I believe that Native Americans have a lot to offer in bringing sanity back into our lives. It is true that we have lost our way through the various policies of the federal government and the Christian missionaries the past two hundred years, however, when we realize that we had one time lived within the circle of the Natural Law, and if we embrace this proven value once again, we can begin to flourish.

The other idea is that the Framers of our Constitution realized that we had to live according to the Law of Nature and Nature's God. It is the coming together, and living by these values, I believe, that we can set our country back on the straight and narrow again. As we speak, we have our politicians trying to solve our national deficit, economic, political and social problems through legislation, when all they need to realize is that these problems are more likely spiritual and moral ones

---

[2] Please see my website www.kadashan.simplesite.com about the Kadashan Family.

and that all we need to do is follow the Natural Law and God's Laws to hash out correct solutions.

The past hundred years have been challenging to us as true blooded Americans. There is a threat that the gradual drifting away from the Constitution has invited the ideas of progressives to infiltrate into our lives. With the advent of western culture invading and changing Native American traditions and customs my people are struggling to regain our presence in a true and great American way. At the very time the progressive movement emerged, the people who had their feet planted firmly were able to send them back into the closet. Today we have as our leaders the sixties, hippy, free loving people who are changing our country very rapidly—and not for the better by a long shot.

Part three in this work are essays about the Alaska Native Brotherhood, the oldest Native American organization in the country. The founders were very traditional, conservative, and wanted the future generation to be worthy Americans. They had a vision for our generation and I thought it would be a good idea for America to become acquainted with the ideas of these visionaries.

This work is dedicated to the young folk who will need to take up the banner of freedom and liberty and to bring back into our lives the safety and protection of constitutional government.[3]

---

[3] See the essay in this work "Something Very Refreshing."

PROLOGUE

Tlingit Values

One of the stories I often share about our Tlingit history is the story about Raven's Creation, at which time I focus on the part where he pulled a large canoe from the ocean.[4] This vessel had animals, fish, birds and wildlife of which the ark had sheltered the animals from the elements; he released them into their future homes between the mountains of Waaseitishaa[5] and Tsalxaan[6] into their future habitat. He removed the house from the canoe and placed it along the banks of the Aaxwei River; this was the beginning of the settlement of the village called Guseix; this would be the first tribal house for the people of Gunaaxoo and was named Far-out House because he had pulled it "far out" from the ocean.

Raven created Gunaaxoo for the Tlingits to migrate to and provide the resources so they could prudently use the things they need to maintain their lives. When the first migrations came to the village of Guseix, Raven instructed the people about how these resources should be taken care of. Each tribal house took care of about fifty people. He told the first settlers that when this house got too small they could use the supplies he created for them to build another home. Eventually

---

[4] See the full account of Raven's creation in the Prologue of my novel When Raven Cries.
[5] Mount Saint Elias (18001 feet—third highest in North America).
[6] Mount Fairweather (15,300 feet)

there were seven houses along the banks of the river. It is evident, through their methods of survival and inner-compass values that they had knowledge of the Natural Law

Raven gave the Tlingit a set of standards to abide by in the beginning, but I believe only a few of the Elders are true to these principles these days, therefore we have a lot of educating to do in these latter days. Most notable of these values are:

1. **Always show reverence to the Creator.** One of the things I've learned about our Maker is that he is the same Creator the Christian missionaries embraced by the Native American of old and Alaska Native peoples.
2. **Respect all life.** Our Raven stories teach that there is life in everything. There is life in the rocks, trees, water, and every material thing. When we show respect to our environment we connect spiritually with Nature therefor Nature has an obligation to provide us with what we need to sustain our lives and foster happiness by our prudent activities.
3. **Don't waste and use everything wisely.** Just good old common sense that everyone should embrace.
4. **Share.** Another common-sense principle—it is evident that in practicing the Law of Nature and God's Laws that when we learn to give, we always get back tenfold.

These standards are based upon the Natural Law. If we violate these ideals—in due time we will begin to see shortages until our precious resources that provide for our livelihood are gone.

After Raven completed his mission, he lost his powers and returned to one even greater than he. This was the Great Spirit who sent Raven and gave him the power to do what he had accomplished on earth.

Where is Raven now? Some people say he went to live on the Nass River where he originally came from. Some think he now lives in a cave near Katella. Tlingit people believe, and look forward to the time, when he will one day return to help mankind remember how to live by the Natural Law once again—much like the people of our heritage—both Native and non-Native.

PART ONE

THEMES FROM SELF GOVERNANCE

"We need to advocate that the <u>restructuring</u> and <u>downsizing</u> of our governments should be <u>right-structuring</u> and <u>right-sizing</u> so that governments can, once again, assume their proper roles in the service to their people."

I am presenting here the American flag with the Indian warrior on the flag to remind us about the influence that the Native Americans had on the Founding Fathers when they were structuring the federal constitutional system.

EARLY AMERICA AND THE NATURAL LAW

In the olden days Native Americans lived with nature. They understood that if you co-existed with nature, you would understand the laws of nature. When we understood the Natural Law we would have the tendency to obey the Natural Law and thus enjoy the privileges the natural world had to offer us. Not only is this true for individuals, but for groups of people, communities, states, and nations as well. This is, even more so, evidently true today. The challenge we have in these modern times, a time when much progress is being made in every way throughout the world, is to return to abiding by the Natural Law.[7]

    I believe that one of the greatest teaching tools for Americans is to embrace what history has to offer, for we have found time and time again that history does, indeed, repeat itself. Many new nations, if looking for freedom and liberty, have formed a government in alignment with some of the Natural Law. They succeeded to a certain extent, and when they fell, it wasn't due to another nation conquering them from without; instead they invariably tumbled due to erosion from within. The American government was formed by men who were able to take the lessons of past civilizations and form a government that evolved into being an ensign to the world. The formula for America's success is incorporated within the pages of the Declaration of Independence and the United States Constitution. As we speak, we see how America

---

[7] See article on Law of Nature and Nature's God in this work

is following the trail of France when it was transforming to complete socialism in the 1840's.[8]

When the explorers first came to the Americas, the aboriginals welcomed them. They believed that these fair skinned people found them to learn how to live by the Natural Law.[9]

The most important learning took place when the Native Americans shared how to live within what I have dubbed a ***land-based economy***. This concept translates to living according to the Natural Law, which encompasses respecting the resources that provide us with life. It is this concept that Alaskan Natives refer to as "our traditional way of life" which is also the basis for the Alaska National Interest Lands and Conservation Act of 1980 (ANILCA) as subsistence. Today America celebrates the survival of the settlers first winter in this land with the Natives—we all know that this is what Thanksgiving is all about.

Despite many trials and challenges for nearly two hundred years, this relationship survived until the colonists began the task of breaking ties from their mother country. We are familiar with the reasons, but some of the main ones were when the mother country committed legal plunder through usurpation and oppression by confiscating property, invading ones private lives, taxation without representation, inability to practice their faiths, etc.[10] As leaders of the rebellion began to emerge, we find that these men were well versed in economics, politics, science, literature, the arts, and, of course, what worked and didn't work with nations that have arisen and disappeared.[11] They also had a positive working relationship with the Iroquois nation. In this day and age it is important to embrace what history has to offer us. There are many lessons we can take from the way nations have risen and fallen. The pattern is pretty much the same. One of these is the idea that mankind has mistakenly repeated over and over is that the government owes us a living. It's important that the true history of America be restored

---

[8] The Law by Frederick Bastiat
[9] Wampum Belts And Peace Trees, Introduction/The Discovery, Page xxiii
[10] Declaration of Independence
[11] Political Writings of W. Cleon Skousen

and taught in the learning institutions. We see in our society today how the progressive movement has been drawn out of the closet and making every effort to discredit the early history of America. For the past hundred years the progressive ideology has been coming in and out of the closet and within the last fifty years have infiltrated into our learning instructions and into our governments. It is these kinds of distraction that steers us from the fundamental concepts that Native Americans knew well, and what this country was based upon.

NATIVE AMERICAN INFLUENCE

Let's offer a brief example of the way Native Americans managed their affairs. When one studies the Confederate Tribes of the Iroquois Nations as an example, one would find that this alliance had a sophisticated structure of government. The Framers of the U.S. Constitution modeled the principles of the confederacy when they began to draft the Articles of Confederation, and later, the U.S. Constitution to form a new government. The Framers became familiar with the tribes in their areas and were intrigued with the structure of the Iroquois Confederacy. They saw within this system a group known as the Fire Keepers, which functioned like the Executive Branch of the U.S Government; then there were the Elder Brothers, a group that functioned like the Senate, and then there were the Younger Brothers, which served in the same capacity as our own house of representatives.[12]

Another concept the colonists used from the Confederacy was how war was determined. Women had a place on tribal councils, and when there was a conflict between tribes, it was the clan mothers who decided whether a tribe should war against another tribe.[13] The offense had to be very serious otherwise thumbs down was given on the idea. The reason why women were allowed to make these decisions was because the male's ego tended to rule his decision making when a tribe offended another tribe. The natural inclination would be to strike back;

---

[12] Wampum Belts And Peace Trees, Chapter three, Page 51
[13] Abide

however, a woman would think more levelheadedly because it would be her husband, son or the young men that would risk their lives in a fracas. If they thought that there was good reason to go to war, then the issue would be delegated to the war chief; it would be his job to lead his men into battle. If there were no good reason for battle, then the problem would be entrusted to the peace chief, whose job it would be to diplomatically settle the dispute. The war chief, then, functions similar to the Secretary of Defense in the American political arena; the peace chief is correlated with the Secretary of State.

Even though these bodies served their purposes in the confederacy, the tribal councils, which originated from the villages, is where the source of important issues originated. In other words, when something of importance had to be addressed it was first brought before the tribal councils, and then it worked its way up the ranking to be considered in the confederation. This important concept Abraham Lincoln understood to mean government of the people, by the people and for the people.

One of the most important things the Founders saw was the benefit of the confederacy, and they used the concept when they formed the thirteen colonies. In fact, because many ideas the Founders incorporated in their deliberations was taken from the Iroquois Confederacy, the Founders original intent was to allow the Confederacy to be included as a fourteenth colony.[14] Indian chiefs, such as White Eyes, were willing to participate in this manner because they believed in the concept of life, liberty and the pursuit of happiness for all people and they fancied that all humankind should live in peace. Communication broke down when word of this was not communicated in time to the frontiers people who were engaged in small battles with the Indians over land claims in the prairies heading west. Also, those like White Eyes was in favor of incorporating the fourteenth colony were getting resistance from both their own people as well as land speculators on the settler's side. In a short time, there was a severe schism between the Founders in Philadelphia and the nearby Indian leaders. When the Revolutionary

---

[14] Wampum Belts And Peace Trees, Chapter Ten, Page 199

War ended, the split was so far apart that the Indians were no longer considered a part of the new America—much less a part of American system of government. Instead they are mentioned in the Commerce Clause of the U.S. Constitution; this interprets, in my opinion, to mean that they would be considered as nations of their own[15] When the Northwest Ordinance was passed by Congress in 1789, this clarified the relationship between U.S. government and the Indian Nations where it said that Indian lands would not be taken without their consent and that their property rights and liberty would never be invaded or disturbed. Treaties became the guiding principle and the adage that treaties were made to be broken took place as the guiding principle and so most treaties were never honored. Prior to the revolution the leaders of early America called the Native Americans their "Brothers." When the idea of the original people becoming a part of the American system had failed, the movement west to take over Indian lands, they began calling them "Children." The commerce clause removed the ability of states to negotiate land and political issues with Indians thereby the first Americans reverted to being wards of the federal government. Being removed from their natural habitat and placed on reservations detached these people from their livelihood. Today they struggle to bring back into their lives the concept of self-governance as they knew it. Aside from broken treaties and having to tolerate early policies that threatened extermination and termination, the Native Americans were able to survive unfair government policies. Even though the Commerce Clause in the U.S. Constitution mentions that we will be treated as nations of our own, tribes were regulated by Congress in ways that prevented them from thriving in their former, natural, environment.[16] Reservation routine, and living according to the Law of Nature, was no longer a part of their lives. When Thomas Jefferson was president he embraced the policy that Native Americans should be assimilated into the new society. Educating the Indian was the key to integrating them into the American system.

---

[15] U.S. Constitution, Article I, Sec. 8, Paragraph 3
[16] The American Indian, Prehistory to the present, Gibson

On the other hand, Andrew Jackson, the infamous Indian fighter, created policies to exterminate the Natives and take over whatever lands that was still in their possession. We all know the ensuing stories that accomplished this.

THE INDIAN REORGANIZATION ACT

In 1934 hope for sovereignty emerged by adoption of the Howard Wheeler Act, now referred to as the Indian Reorganization Act. Felix S. Cohen, an expert on Indian law, wrote an article that appeared in the publication called the "American Indian" in 1949. In his opening paragraph he makes a timely statement, which embodies all that man has striven for since time immemorial. It also perfectly aligns with the idea that we all have a natural right—a natural desire—to govern ourselves. He wrote:

> "**Not all who speak of self-government mean the same thing by the term. Therefore, let me say at the outset that by self-government I mean that form of government in which decisions are made not by the people who are wised, or ablest, or closest to some throne in Washington or in heaven, but rather by the people who are most directly affected by the decisions.**"

Here Cohen emphasizes that decisions affecting people should be made by the people themselves, and then when further assistance, like the Iroquois structure, is needed it is taken up the ladder. True influence comes from the bottom rather than from the top down, as it is practiced by the government today.

Lucy Kramer Cohen, wife of Felix, made an interesting statement about her husband. She wrote:

> **"Felix wrote some papers when he was in college about the Indians and it was likely our nation of democracy came from Benjamin Franklin having been ambassador to the Iroquois Confederacy in 1763."**[17]

This is what was proficient in the early days of the republic. However Indian tribes were taken out of this loop when they were made wards of the government. When the termination area came into being, the federal government took over trust responsibility for tribes, meaning that they would remain guardians of federal dogmas until such a time when tribes would be able to take control of their own destinies. This was what the Indian Reorganization Act was supposed to do. However, because of the lack of human resources on reservations, tribal leader's hands were tied as far as developing themselves on an economic basis;[18] so they held onto this trust responsibility obligation for dear life.

In Alaska the Indian Reorganization Act did not apply on the onset of its passing because there were no reservations in Alaska.[19] If an Alaskan community wanted to take advantage of the Act it had to be a reservation, or request reservation status.[20] This was during the time when Alaska Native leaders in southeast Alaska were struggling with getting Native Alaskans recognized as citizens. Many of our young people were sent to boarding schools in the "south forty-eight" for their education, where they became acquainted with their counter-parts from the reservations. After they visited the reservations, they came back

---

[17] Indian Self Rule, page 70, Howe Brothers, Salt Lake city Utah
[18] The American Indian, Prehistory to the present, Gibson
[19] The Native Brotherhoods: Modern Intertribal Organization On the Northwest Coast, Pages 52-53
[20] Abide

home dead set against the idea of reservation status.²¹ These people wanted to be recognized as U.S. citizens, and to accept reservation status, they felt, would be a step backward.²² In 1936 Congress amended the Indian Reorganization Act so the IRA's could become applicable to Alaska. There were feeble attempts to take advantage of it.²³ It wasn't until recent years that the Indian Reorganization Act has become an issue among tribes in Alaska; only it is on a more positive note, and federally recognized tribes are using it to achieve more self-governance for their villages.

In the 1971 the Indian Self-Determination and Education Act (PL 93-638) was passed by Congress. This made it possible for tribes to take on more responsibilities for themselves, particularly around education. The rationale here, returned to President Jefferson's idea, was when Indian people became educated and trained they would be able to work toward self-sufficiency. The trust responsibility, however, of the federal government to tribes were still intact. Again, tribes held onto this trust responsibility concept for dear life in the fear that their funding would be in jeopardy of being consistent. In time the so-called "638 contracting" became such a bureaucratic nightmare to where it was becoming nearly impossible for tribes to receive their federal funding in a timely manner. Despite untiring efforts to try and resolve problems with the BIA, the Bureau was unwilling to change its function as a service provider and manager of tribal affairs to an administrator of government contracts. One effort to reform the BIA was Section 209, which Congress made as an addendum to the Indian Self Determination and Education Assistance Act. This was initiated by the Department of Interior and the issue would have provided direct transfer of services to the tribal level with a waiver of trust responsibility of the United States Government. This issue did not meet well with tribes because of the trust responsibility issue. So, tribes began to

---

²¹ Abide
²² The Native Brotherhoods: Modern Intertribal Organizations On the Northwest Coast, P.51
²³ Public Law No, 538, 74th Congress

assemble, first as a small group, to fathom out solutions for the BIA to deliver its functions, services, programs and activities in a more effective and efficient manner. Thus, became Title III, PL 100-472 which we now know of as the Self Governance Demonstration Project.

The law now required Congress to establish, in the federal bureaucracy, an Office of Self Governance for tribes. This was initiated by tribal leaders who felt there needed to be a mechanism for tribes to become self-sufficient. So, Congress, through a tribally driven initiative, passed this legislation with the intent to place more responsibility onto tribes. In June of 1991 the elder President Bush made this statement:

> **"An office of Self-Governance has been established in the Department of Interior and given the responsibility of working with tribes to craft creative ways of transferring decision-making powers over tribal government functions from the department to tribes."**

The purpose for the self-governance initiative was to <u>restructure</u> and <u>downsize</u> the Bureau of Indian Affairs, and transfer more programs, functions, services and activities to the individual tribal level. Whatever funding that was attached to these would also be transferred as well. At first the Bureau of Indian Affairs resisted the self-governance concept. It took nearly four years before it realized that self-governance was not going to go away. In fact, self-governance grew so rapidly among tribes across the nation that a snow balling effect of tribes was interring into self-governance; today about half of the tribes are now what is called compacting (self-governing) tribes. In 1994 the demonstration project became permanent and that same year the Indian Health Service started a Self-Governance Demonstration Project. HUD has also followed suit and other agencies are also making attempts to mirror the self-governance idea.

Danny Jordon, one of the instigators of the self-governance idea, made this statement, **"We need to advocate that the <u>restructuring</u> and <u>downsizing</u> of our governments should be <u>right-structuring</u>**

and right-sizing so that governments can, once again, assume their proper roles in the service to their people." I advocate that this idea should apply not only to tribal governments, but to federal, state, and local governments as well.

NON-BIA PROGRAMS

In April of 1994 President Clinton signed an Executive Order[24] which directed all federal agencies to begin working with tribal governments on a "real" government-to-government relationship. In relation to that directive, later that year Ada Deere, Assistant Secretary of Interior, was authorized to announce the Non-BIA Programs.

This clarified President Clinton's directive and identified what those agencies under the Department of Interior were obligated to do in their relationship with tribes. The purpose for the Non-BIA project was to allow federal agencies to enter into self-governance relationship with federally recognized tribes. If an agency had any programs, functions, services or activities that had historical, cultural or geographical significance to a tribe, then that agency would be obligated to allow tribes to use their compacting powers to negotiate a Funding Agreement for the tribe to take over that program, function, service or activity. Even though this was a directive from the President of the United States, leaders in the agencies, like the Bureau of Indian Affairs and National Parks Service, were resisting releasing the power, control and funding to tribes who have made attempts to work with these agencies. Today, tribal leaders have thrown their hands up, frustrated because these agencies were unwilling to cooperate. As of this date only five tribes have compacting agreements with the non-BIA agencies. Some things

---

[24] American Indian/Alaska Native Policy, Memorandum For The Heads of Executive Departments and Agencies

have been done, however, like the Fish and Wild Life Service has entered into co-operative or co-management agreements with tribes in Alaska. This is not, in any measure of our imagination, self-governance. Larger tribes and tribal organizations like the Alaska Inter-Tribal Council and National Congress of American Indians will have to keep this idea of self-governance, particularly the Non-BIA Programs, alive and assist tribes toward making this concept a reality.

Having these brought to the tribal, or local level, will make it possible for tribes to advance themselves politically, economically and socially as well as allowing decision making and management abilities to be given to those people of whom they are affected by the most.

USDA (FOREST SERVICE) DEMONSTRATION PROJECT

Because the U.S. Forest Service is under the Department of Agriculture it wasn't included in the announcement made by Ada Deer's Non-BIA Programs, however President Clinton's directive did include them when he said that <u>all federal</u> agencies must begin working with tribes on a government-to-government relationship. Even though the Forest Service functions under the policies of the Department of Agriculture, it has taken some important steps to begin working with tribes on a government- to-government relationship. However, they have never made any gestures toward self-governance. Soon after President Clinton's directive was made public, the Forest Service began developing a ***National Resource Book on American Indian and Alaska Native Relations.*** The book was published to train their personnel on how to work with tribal organizations and federally recognized tribes. The Forest Service has made some progress in working with tribes and is constantly working toward Memorandums of Understanding/Agreements and interring into co-operative agreements with tribes; however, there is still a lack of willingness to allow tribes to become self-governing because the central government is claiming what they call inherent rights to retain certain functions, services and activities for themselves. This trust responsibility has taken a reverse angle, and until tribes are willing to continually emphasize this idea of self-governance, tribes will be content with just being co-managers of programs, services, functions and activities that really belong at a local level. Self-governance is a Natural Law concept that the Founding Fathers of America emphasized as important in the Declaration of Independence and in the U.S. Constitution.

Self-governance, like freedom, must constantly be fought for, not only among tribal leaders, but leaders in our states and local governmental agencies as well. This is an American issue and we should all come together and bring the fundamentals of the power of local governments, and American ideals, back together again.

THE DECLARATION OF INDEPENDENCE AND THE U.S. CONSTITUTION LIMITS GOVERNMENT

Let us, now, examine some of the concepts and principles contained in the Declaration of Independence and in the U.S. Constitution in its original form. The second paragraph of the Declaration of Independence states that:

> "We hold these truths to be self-evident, that all men are created equal, that they are endowed by their <u>creator</u> with certain unalienable rights, that among these are life, liberty and the pursuit of happiness. That to secure these rights governments are instituted among men, <u>deriving their just powers from the consent of the governed</u>. That whenever any form of government becomes destructive of these ends, it is the right of the people to alter or to <u>abolish</u> it, and to <u>institute a new government</u>, laying its foundation on such principles and organizing its powers in such form, as to them shall seem most likely to affect their safety and happiness."

The Declaration emphasizes that the purpose of government is to protect its citizens. This means that our lives, our liberties, and our pursuit of happiness must be safeguarded, and secured for all citizens under the umbrella of the federal government. However, what this paragraph means is that should the federal government ever arrive at a point where it no longer does these—that is protect our lives, secure our liberties, and no longer guarantees our pursuit of happiness, then it is up to the American people to alter or abolish that government and start a new one based on those same principles—that is the protection of our lives, our liberties, etc.

The Declaration also states that the powers of governments come from the consent of the governed. This means that under this system of government the Founders embraced the concept that good people elect exemplary people to represent them in the affairs of government. These elected representatives are delegated to do what the normal person on the street cannot do for himself, and anything more or less than the protection of our lives, liberties and pursuit of happiness is either usurpation or oppression. It also means that no law can be made unless the people consent to it. That's where public hearings and local entities can be effective. But the people we put into office to represent us are failing to listen to the citizenry. What has happened within the last century, more so during the last half— and even more-so in the last decade—is that the government has grown so large that many of the rights of individuals have been either usurped or oppressed.

Article IV, Section 4 of the Constitution says that states are guaranteed a Republican Form of Government. What this means is that the federal government will be limited in what it could do and is implied that most of the services would be supplied by the states and local governments. This also means that we would enjoy a representative form of government, which means that states and the people from the respective states would elect senators and representative to look after our best interests, not their best interests. Whatever happened to President Bill Clinton's statement after his second term election that the days of big government is over?

Today, we have become accustomed to the idea that government should take care of us, when in fact it is our duty to see that government doesn't get involved in doing so much that we become dependent upon it for our very existence. This is what happened to the Native Americans after they were placed on reservations and became wards of the federal government. Having been moved from their fertile environments and deprived of the ability to thrive from their lands, and live under their own banner of freedom, their lifestyle was immediately shifted from a people of self-sufficiency to dependency—reliance on "big brother" to provide for all their needs. In time, if this type of management continues, the American citizenry will also become wards of the federal government.

In Article I, Section 8, Paragraph 3 of the Constitution reference is made regarding the regulation of commerce. It says that Congress shall have the power **"To regulate commerce with foreign nations, and among the several States, and with the Indian tribes."** Some people will contend that tribes should be treated the same as foreign nations, others would argue that they should be regarded the same as states. However, as we examine laws over the past hundred years Congress has passed, we have seen in Alaska the effort to terminate tribes and move toward putting them under the respective state jurisdiction. A most recent effort was to place them under regional corporations whereby funding would be given to the corporations and filtered to tribes according to what they needed.

It's important to address the Alaska Native issue a well. For the past two hundred years the Alaska Native peoples were driven from a hearty, self-reliant, lofty heritage.[25] Then when outside influences came (here's that NATURE within the circle idea again), the people's lives slowly transpired to dependency on government to take care of us. Even today, we relish the good old times and talk about how our ancestors provided for themselves as well as had the ability to govern their affairs through their tribal councils. They depended on the Creator, and themselves, to show them ways in which to live and survive from a harsh environment.

---

[25] Alaska Native Commission Final Report

We talk about these things and wish we could go back to those days but, ironic enough, at the same time we hold our hands out for more federal aid because we have become accustomed to "big brother" taking care of us. We need to remember that, as true Americans, we should not let government do too much for us that we become dependent on "big brother" for our very survival.

THE POWER TO TAX

Before we go any further, I think it would be important to talk about this issue of taxation. It is probably one of the greatest ills that have been imposed on us by the federal government; although it was introduced to the American people during a time of great need I think it is necessary to address how it came about and how the Founding Fathers felt about it. Thomas Jefferson believed that the power to tax is the power to destroy. Chief Justice of the Supreme Court, Earl Warren, had to deal with his issue during his time and felt the same way. What these men really meant was that to give the power to the central government to tax on our incomes would become potentially demeaning to the souls of the American people. So, the Constitution, in its original form, never provided for the federal government to impose a direct tax on the American people's income. After all, one of the reasons why the colonists broke away from their mother country was because of this issue of taxing the settlers without representation. After long debate between the Republicans and Democrats in Congress, the Sixteenth Amendment to the Constitution provided for the federal government to institute the graduated, or direct, income tax. The Sixteenth Amendment was ratified by the states in February of 1913. Up to that time the federal government's ability to tax the American laborer was, indeed, unconstitutional; taxation in this manner was reserved only for the states and local governments. Prior to the Sixteenth Amendment states contributed to the federal treasury according to that state's population.[26]

---

[26] U.S. Constitution, Article I, Sec. 2, Paragraph 3

What happened after this was gradual. It was during the depression that the American people realized what the federal government can do to better serve them. An increase in taxing was supposed to be only temporary until private businesses were able get back on their feet; Social Security, for instance, was supposed to phase out when the insurance companies were strengthened and back on their feet; instead services from the federal level increased until now some people (liberals and progressives) adamantly believe that we can redistribute wealth through the taxing system. This system never worked because it has proven so from the history of nations that have come and gone—one of the main reasons for their fall was that people got the impression that they could live off the government. Contributing to a central fund and then attempting to redistribute the wealth corrupts, and as some of the opponents of the sixteenth amendment said, "Will make a nation of liars." Today, we attend conventions, conferences and meetings to strategize how we can have a larger cut of the federal pie.

How, then, did the federal government finance its services? The states contributed into the central treasurer based on their population to finance any issues that had national significance, like defense, transportation between states, etc. It also lived off the tariff and excise taxes from trade with foreign countries, etc. The issue of building and strengthening the economies was left to local entities and to the states. [27] Today the federal government collects most of the taxes from our incomes and redistributes from a leaky pot. Ideas from abolishing the IRS to imposing a flat or national sales tax are immerging as solutions to our over-taxing problem.

I believe that state and local governments should be able to adequately handle our fiscal affairs. Prosperity begins with the individual and absorbed by the community which in turn is forwarded to the state; when the state prospers a portion of its excesses is contributed to the federal coffers. [28]

---

[27] The Federalist Papers
[28] See The Power to Tax the Power to Destroy in this work

WHO SHOULD OWN LAND?

An example of the federal government taking over many things that belong to the states and local governments, and to the people, is this issue of land. Article I, Section 8, Paragraph 17 of the U.S. Constitution gives no authority for the central government to hold or own land without the <u>consent</u> of the <u>respective Legislatures of the States</u>. The only land the constitution authorizes the government to own are those areas they can use for the central seat of government not exceeding ten miles square, the erection of forts, magazines, arsenals, dockyards and "other needful buildings." The drafters of the Constitution only intended the federal government to manage the land where it had jurisdiction; the lands really belong to the states and to the people. Yet the federal government, through executive orders by some Presidents, under the stewardship of the Forest Service, the National Parks Service and Bureau of Land Management are the largest land barons in the country.

The Native Allotment Act and Homestead Act should be compared here. During the termination era, if an American Indian, or an Alaskan Native, did not want to be a part of a reservation system, then they had an option of becoming individual land owners through the Native Allotment Act passed by Congress in 1906. However, there was a major stumbling block with this proposal. If a Native had a claim on a certain piece of land, he or she had to prove that they, or a family member, occupied that property prior to 1906; however, under the Homestead

Act, all a non-native had to do was squat on a piece of property for seven years and they would gain title to 160 acres of land. It is much easier for a non-native to gain title to land than it is for a genuine Native American. Today there is a proposal in the hands of the Alaska Congressional Delegation to mandate the U.S. Congress change the prior use requirement to "ancestral" use. This would open a host of closed allotment to be reopened and placed in pending status thereby allowing it to go through the process of getting those terminated allotments certified.[29]

The governments taking over these kinds of land are contrary to another Natural Law concept which the Constitution states that "every person has the right to own, develop, and dispose of property."

---

[29] State of Alaska Legislature Joint Resolution 27, 2006.

THE CONCEPT OF STATE'S RIGHTS

Another issue that needs to be addressed is State's Rights. The concept of State's Rights was borrowed from the Confederate Tribes of the Iroquois.[30] The Confederation felt that they should not interfere with the issues within the individual tribes because they knew that the best solutions would come from those people most affected by it. The Seventeenth Amendment to the Constitution eroded states' rights and as a result transferred more control onto the federal government. Before the Seventeenth Amendment was ratified, senators from the states were appointed by the state legislatures. The senator's job was then to look after the best interest of their respective state legislatures. The representatives, on the other hand, were elected by the people from their states and their job was to look after the best interest of the people. The Seventeenth Amendment changed how senators were to serve. They are now to be elected by the people from their respective states. This changed how they should, and who they should, serve. As a result, State's Rights today are ignored and, because of this, many adverse things have prevented people from managing and benefiting from their natural resources because the federal government now has the ability to own and regulate land. It is true that the lands belong to the American people, however the original intent of the U.S. Constitution was to have states and local governments retain control and management of their lands within their

---

[30] Wampum Belts And Peace Trees

respective boundaries.[31] It stands to reason that whoever has control of land has control of the natural resources. Keeping this control local and under state jurisdiction will enable benefactors to determine their own destinies and promote the economic development and wellbeing of the people. Now today, as mentioned earlier, the federal government owns and controls most of the land in the nation—in Alaska, for instance, 66 percent of the land is federally controlled 22% by people and corporations.

This immense control is depriving the state from managing its own resources. This is, indeed, contrary to an important element derived from the Natural Law concept that every free man should have the right to self-government.

---

[31] Action For Americans, The Liberty Amendment, Page 40

ALTERING OR ABOLISHING GOVERNMENTS

The Declaration of Independence has a clause in it that tells how the American people can alter or abolish governments. It was inserted here by the Founders to serve as a last resort when the people think that a government gets too oppressive. The fifth article of the Constitution empowers Congress, with two thirds of both houses, to propose amendments to the Constitution. If Congress doesn't, or won't do it, the issue can revert to the states at which time they can call such a thing as a constitutional convention. At this time amendments can be proposed to submit to Congress. If we are honest in our desire to bring governments into their proper, natural, perspectives, this would be a good idea to consider this course of action at this time.

First, I think a good place to start is to resurrect the Liberty Amendment that has been lingering in Congress since 1933. It addresses all the issues that I have been writing about for the past years in my Juneau Empire column. What the amendment will do is take the government out of competing with private enterprises, turn the lands it has control over back to states and to the people, and do away with the federal income tax. With the possibility of a new congress coming in 2014, it would be a good time to resurrect the Liberty Amendment, because it addresses how the ills of this country can be solved and the government brought back under constitutional law.[32]

---

[32] Mark Levin has a new book called the Liberty Amendment. I support his idea that a constitutional convention should be called by the states to propose an

Second, it is incumbent that we continue to exercise our natural right to self-government in our own communities. Not only should we, as Native Americans and Alaska Natives, bring back the principle of local control, but it is equally incumbent for that all Americans to do the same. To alter the federal system will take a concerted effort on all peoples who live under the banner of the U.S. Constitution because when things start traversing in the wrong direction it is our right to do so.

Third, it is important that local entities work, and develop, their management plans for their own resources; it is even more important to manage these ourselves. Federal programs, as we know them today, will have to be brought back to local control. This idea was practiced in the early days of the republic and Felix Cohen understood it as an important element in tribal self-governance. Not only should Native Americans and Alaska Natives continually battle for this right, but it should be made an American initiative as well. This will be a formidable task, but freedom was never accomplished by people sitting on the fence waiting for something to happen.

Fourth, the state of Alaska is going to have to recognize tribal governments. No matter how cumbersome this might seem to the state leaders, the legislature is going to have to accept the fact that long before they ever came about, tribal governments existed in various forms, and should be recognized again. A tradeoff is that tribes, through their regional organizations, and as individual tribes, can advocate for states' rights. After all, the idea came from Native Americans anyway. Why not bring it back?

Fifth, we must work together (Native and nonnative) to make sure that land ownership is brought back to the people and to the states. As the State of Alaska gains control of land, then it will be able to determine how property rights should be utilized and/or developed. The state will, in turn, must assist all closed Native Allotments be reopened and certified, so that Natives will be able to use these holdings to their benefit in whatever way they see most fitting. An appeal to the

---

Amendment that will bring state's right back and to the people.

Secretary of Interior would be the first step in this effort; if the Secretary is unable to decide, then it should be brought before Congress. [33] An act of Congress will probably be the ultimate way to solve this issue in the long run. Once the state has recognized tribal governments and assisted in this land issue, then these would be able to operate under state charters. With a land base, the people of Alaska will be able to prosper and build a strong economic base for themselves, the state, and make a compelling contribution to the nation as well.

Sixth, Alaska Regional and Village ANSCA Corporations should fit themselves into the scheme of things together. This remains to be discussed further by people involved, however if these corporations were to be made a part of the Alaska's Indian Country, you can see the economic boost that can result for Native Alaskans. Power and control will not need to be fought for—I believe -it will come naturally and a have positive effect on the overall progress of Alaska. The federal dole will largely be eliminated and pride in the people of Alaska will have been achieved. What better way is there to reduce the national debt, and keep the federal budget lean and balanced? That trust responsibility will fade away by itself and I sincerely believe that no one will feel the difference.

Seventh, for a short-term resolve, it should be a priority to promote the self-governance concept in the federal agencies. We should not give up on the Non-BIA Programs. The secret to making this happen is to educate those agencies on what their obligations are to America's citizens. Even though this initiative was driven by tribal governments, this movement will work for local municipalities as well.

Eighth, Tribes should start a tribally driven initiative to get the USDA to allow the Forest Service to do a self-governance demonstration project. This will follow the example that the Bureau of Indian Affairs did when it went into a demonstration project. Local governments should work together and support one another on these issues. Once

---

[33] In 2006 the Alaska Legislature passed Joint Resolution 27 petitioning Congress to reopen all closed Native and Veterans allotment claims and see them toward certification.

these programs, functions, services and activities have been brought to a local level, then those that will be able to do so should be made self-sustaining. This is, perhaps, one way the federal government can free itself from its trust responsibility.

Once Natives are confident that they can take responsibility for their own destinies, and are reliant on their own efforts, I think that there will eventually be no reliance on the federal government. I believe this can very much set the pace for the rest of this great country to achieve the vision of a pre-colonial and very wise tribal leader, Sachem Netawatwees; his desire for all people of the Americas was to enjoy life, liberty and pursuit of happiness including all peoples from sea to shining sea.

OUR PROBLEMS ARE UNIVERSAL PROBLEMS

The problems that Native American and Alaska Natives are facing are not only confined to our communities and our own lives; they are universal problems. They are the same problems shared by other ethnic groups in America. In our attempt to solve these problems in the political arena we fail to recognize that the real issues are spiritual and moral ones. That is why it is important for us as Native Americans to begin abiding by the Law of Nature and Nature's God. History has proven that when mankind's spirituality has eroded, his religious strength is weakened, and when spirituality is gone so goes the potency of the family unit, then the village, the community, the state and then the nation.

Our people lived secure, healthy and prosperous lifestyles before; we can do it again. When we find ways to do this, then we have an obligation to share it with our brothers and sisters in our communities, our state, our nation and the world because truth does, indeed, belong to everyone.

PART TWO

THE LAW OF NATURE

"—our perception is that if you do not operate around the real laws of the universe, you are challenging fundamental cycles that you depend on for life."

Chief Oren Lyons (Onondaga)

THE LAW OF NATURE AND NATURE'S GOD

When I was a very young man I subscribed to a book club that enabled me to obtain the writings and thoughts of great men from the past. One of these men was Marcus Tullius Cicero (104-43 B.C.) who was a Roman philosopher and political writer. He believed that there were ideologies that all mankind must abide by. It is called the Natural Law.

Cicero explained that Natural Law was the Creator's order of things—that it is true law and that true law is right reason in agreement with nature. He also said that it is immoral to try to alter it, repeal it or abolish it; he stated that "We cannot be freed of its obligations by senate or people." He also revealed that, "It is one eternal and unchangeable law that will be valid for all nations and all times."

One of my favorite modern-day political thinkers, and writer, is the late W. Cleon Skousen. Skousen advanced this Natural Law idea further. He agreed with Cicero that God's law is, indeed, "right reason" however he said, "when perfectly understood is wisdom— and when applied to government it translates to justice." I subscribe to these thoughts and know that the Founders also indorsed the Natural Law as well. It is stated in the first paragraph of the Declaration of Independence; read where it addresses that we should abide by the Law of Nature and Nature's God. It would be well to recognize that the Natural Law has been with us since the recorded history of mankind. Many great nations that have come and gone rose to their grandeur by abiding by the sound principles and fell when they drifted from them. The pilgrims realized that the Native Americans lived within the laws of nature when they came to our lands and spent their first winter with them. The Natives assisted the new-comers with schemes on how to survive their first winter and were introduced to living within the circle of the Natural Law. Our U.S. Constitution was founded upon the Natural Law and god's commandments. Compare, if you will, the Ten Commandments and the statutes found in our own government. The "thou shalt not's" are the same.

On August 13, 2009 I remember President Obama having a town hall meeting in Montana. Near the end of his presentation a young lady read the Preamble of the Montana Constitution and acknowledged the President as a constitutional scholar; she then challenged him to read the rest of that state's constitution. It is true that Obama received his degree from Harvard University in constitutional law, but I have been appalled about how he is ignoring our own U.S. Constitution. The Montana woman should have challenged him to read it most of all. It is difficult for me to accept any proof that he supports the very instrument that allowed him to become our President.

I am disturbed at the lack of interest that people in government have in the U.S. Constitution of which principles in it are based on Natural Law and the Laws of God. I hear the common person on the street say that we need to go back to the Constitution. I also have heard people say that the Constitution needs to be changed to fit the changing times. And yet there are some who believe that the Constitution is out dated and should be replaced. This is pretty much in affect because many of our politicians are completely ignoring it. I believe that the Founders created a living document that will stand the test of time—because of human nature and the Natural Law and Nature's God doctrine.

But how do we change our course of thinking to restoring these principles, so we do not have to go the ways of those nations that have benefited from their governments founded on those laws and eventually forsook them? Well we could take a lesson from the "tea party" movement, and make our voices heard whenever we can—but we also need to be well versed in the document that the Founding Fathers put a lot of faith in when it was ratified.

Article IV, Section 4 of the Constitution says that every state shall be guaranteed a republican form of government. This means that our governments will be representative in nature and limited to what it can do. This, likewise, means that good people elect virtuous people to represent their best interests in government. They are our servants and work for us. If they don't do what their constituents want them to do, then they no longer are servants but the "know-it-all's" and think that they are the beyond listening to the people. That is, of course, until it comes time for reelections. In connection to this, the 10th Amendment to the Constitution addresses the fact that all powers come from the people through the states and are then delegated to the federal government. Ever read that part in the Declaration where it references the fact that the people who administer the affairs of government receive their powers from the "consent of the governed?" This means that no law should be made without the stamp of approval of the people. Town hall meetings are important, and our legislatures should listen to the people when they voice their opinion. Tea party movements are legitimate as well and should be applauded instead of down-played.

Another example of a Natural Law is found in the Declaration of Independence which emphasizes that the federal government shouldn't do anything that would deprive us of our liberties, safety for our lives, and our pursuit of happiness.[34] For these reasons, this unique government was instituted for our benefit. Governments should follow this irreplaceable law by guaranteeing us our right to say or write what we want without being persecuted by government, factions of parties, or special interest groups. Our governments should be guaranteed the safety of our lives so that we can go to work, to school, for a walk or a run in the park, without being shot at, abused, kidnapped or held hostage. The pursuit of happiness is a natural desire of mankind and when mentioned in the Declaration it permits us to do whatever we

---

[34] Please look forward to what "happiness" in this context in a future writing.

want to do to make us happy so long as we do not interfere with the right of another person from doing the same thing.

The Declaration also declares that when governments no longer does these things, then it is up to us—the American people—to either alter or abolish that government and start a new one based on those same principles—that is the protections of our lives, our liberties, and our pursuits of happiness. These principles are grounded from the Natural Law; when we stray from those values bad things happen, like the bye-gone days of great nations that have crumbled into oblivion.

W. Cleon Skousen, in his book The 5000 Year Leap, emphasizes that the United States was designed by the Founders for a moral people. Alexis Tocqueville, in his book Democracy in America, said that "America is great because America is good." Then as an afterthought he said, "America will cease to be great only when it ceases to be good."

It's time to awaken that "sleeping giant" within us and start restoring our living Constitution and proven values that made America a great nation! Not only should we give deference to the Law of Nature, but we should value God's laws with equal devotion. This concept in the declaration reminds us that this country was founded on faith in the Creator. When we study early American history we find that religion was an important part in the people's daily living. When we become more familiar with the Natural Law and Nature's God, we may learn that the laws of nature and God's laws are the same. I believe that we have an obligation and duty to educate ourselves on these issues. Just as important we should make sure that correct American history is taught in the schools. Will Durant, in his history book, Our Oriental Heritage admonish us to leave a legacy for the future:

"Let us, before we die, gather up our heritage, and offer it to our children."

So, should it be for our day and age.

THE SPECTRUM OF THE CONSTITUTIONAL EAGLE

September 21, 2009

I was once asked by a close relative what political party I belonged to. "Well," I said, "I like to consider myself a political isolationist. However, I've had the experience of belonging to both parties."

Her next question was, "Does your mother know about this?"

I have to admit I was somewhat appalled at what I thought about my mother having to approve of my political preference. My relation regarded herself as a staunch democrat, so she assumed that my mother was a democrat too. She thought that anything more or less than that for me would be a sin.

"Sometime," I said to her, "I will explain to you why I am what I am."

So, next of kin, here goes.

When you think about it, in actuality one cannot really tell what a democrat or a republican stand for these days. For decades many people have been losing faith in these two key political parties. We hear the terms liberal and conservative as unscrupulous individuals and then they tend to become the subjects of condemnation with whichever party is in control, whether it be in the state or national governments. Our real fear should be in the progressive movement because they include politicians from both political parties.

When I was trying to understand everything during my younger years I choose to be a democrat when I decided to get politically active.

My father and mother were staunch democrats and I, too, took the view that anything more or less than that for me would be a sin. President John F. Kennedy was in office then and I must admit that I was a loyal admirer of this man; it deeply affected me when he was assassinated. However, in hindsight, what smacked me even more was when I heard his inaugural speech. I was especially caught when he said, "Ask not what your country can do for you, ask what you can do for your country." I was in college then and I actually stood up and cheered.

"At last," I said to a friend who would later be a liberal. "This country is coming to its own!"

In later years, I would understand by retrospection how, during his brief tenure, his administration had been responsible for congressional bills that did exactly the opposite.

However, on the onset, I once again cheered when I witnessed head start and general assistance programs come into our community.

"At last," I said again, "this country is coming to its own." This chant, I realized years later, was one of the main reasons why great nations that have vanished because people had begun to think that their government owed them a living.

Then Kennedy was assassinated; Lyndon Johnson succeeded him. What Kennedy was unable to finish, Johnson's Great Society brought about: more welfare-like programs. I saw what it was doing to the people in small villages and impoverished communities. I witnessed competent people in my community becoming more dependent upon the dole— like some of my buddies forsaking the opportunity to work, fish harder, or try to remain self-sufficient because of the attitude that the "Government will take care of me." I realized then that if we stayed on this course our culture would vanish, so I began to rethink seriously about this kind of viewpoint. The ideas of the day really didn't agree with my inner compass feelings.

I lived far back enough to see how the generation of my parents and grandparents suffered hardships, but the government wasn't there to pull them out of their dilemmas. During the runs of the salmon in the summer, people worked hard to catch the fish they needed to survive the long winter months; and so they practiced what their ancestors had been proficient with since time immemorial—that of surviving off the land—a term we know today as a subsistence lifestyle. When we fished in the Akwe River during the summer my father made sure that we separated several salmon from our commercial catch for personal use. We smoked and fresh packed the salmon for the long winter months. Also, during the berry seasons my mother took us to the strawberry patches along the ocean shores between the Akwe River and Dry Bay. Then we picked salmon and blueberries across the river from our fish camp. These were enjoyed during the season, but my mother also jarred these for the winter months. In the coolness of long winter, there were times when the children went to the Opher Creek, a mile or so out of town, and speared red fish for the dinner table. I remember my dad and his brother going halibut fishing in the cold of the winter—especially during the month of March—to provide fresh fish.[35] Winter king salmon was also a delicacy. Hunting seal, another good source of protein for our bodies, was hunted— the fat rendered and used for dipping dried salmon. Deer was not plentiful but was shot when opportunity presented itself. The work was hard, and people had to be willing to put forth the effort— or starve.

In February we kids had fun dip netting for candle fish along the sandy shore at the head of Monti Bay; we would deliver them to the elders and enjoy these deep fried like French fries. Later, in March, the hooligans showed up in the Situk River, ten miles distance, and the men would pull their sleds out there and bring back hundreds of pounds of these little delicacies for the community.

In the sixties when some of the older people began to "walk into the forest," and the young minds of the day were giving into getting something for nothing, I began to re-evaluate my political way of thinking.

So, I became a republican.

So what?

---

[35] In March of 1947 my uncle, Henry Adams and his friend Norman (Blackie) Lott, both drowned while jigging for halibut across the bay from the village of Yakutat. Their bodies were never recovered.

That was my right, wasn't it?

I hoped that my mother, who was still living, didn't hold that against me.

I did some research on what the GOP's basic philosophy stood for—like advocating for retaining our traditions (I now understood why it was called the Grand Ole Party) and keeping the government out of our lives (I began to understand where President Reagan was coming from). These concepts appealed to my inner compass and so I began to hang onto them for dear life.

I finished college late in life, and although I didn't major in political science or government, I did take a cavernous interest in American history. I was an English major and when I was accepted into this discipline, one of my professors commented that English literature was the "conscience of the college campuses." I'm not sure whether he was trying to make me feel privileged at the time; all I was interested in was learning how to write effectively. Now I understand that he meant an English Literature major is able to discover things from any of the disciplines. If there was any one thing that I learned as a college student is was that one can, if he or she is serious, learn how to learn. Another thing I learned was to become an independent thinker and that we don't have to—shouldn't have to—follow the popular trends of the day if we don't believe that they would be detrimental to our health and well-being.

Over the years, because I did, indeed, learn how to learn, I became interested in many things. Politics being one of them, I learned that there is this concept the Founders called the Constitutional Eagle. On this spectrum the right half of the wing represents the conservative philosophy and the other the liberal. Conservatives believe in a strict interpretation of the Constitution, stressing that the less government is the best, while liberals have a loose interpretation advocating that government has the answers to all our dilemmas. The vision the early leaders of this nation had was that the American voters would be able to bring these two concepts toward the middle and be able to serve in the best interest of the American people. You see, it is really up to us, the voters, to make sure the country is run right by who we put into these offices. Sometimes the liberals would have the upper hand; other times the conservatives would prevail. The electorates, indeed, should speak by the condition of the times using the Constitution and Natural Law as guides.

The President however—according to the wishes of the Founders—is to govern from the middle. Jefferson had a strong view that it was the role of the President to not allow the central government to drift too far on either side of the spectrum. It matters not whether he is republican or democrat, conservative or liberal, his job is to honor, support and defend the Constitution of the United States. He said in his publication *The Writings of Thomas Jefferson:*

"These men have no right to office. If a monarchist be in office, anywhere, and it be known to the President, the oath he has taken to support the Constitution imperiously require the instantaneous dismissing of such officer; and I hold the President criminal if he be permitted such to remain—"

And so, when you listen to a democrat or a republican talk, try to decipher how they view the Constitution. I'm sure you'll be, like me, disappointed with many on both sides. You'll probably find, as I have, that many of our candidates, or people in offices, are more party orientated than constitutionally aligned. This, indeed, presents a danger to the political arena in America in that the politicians are more interested in getting your votes so he or she can stay in their positions to retain power and control.

Instead today our so-called public servants are more party orientated rather than constitutionally aligned. For instance, Bill Clinton proclaimed during his campaign that he was a faithful Jeffersonian Democrat. If so, then why didn't he follow one important concept Thomas Jefferson warned the American people about regarding the power to tax? Jefferson wrote in his book entitled WORKS: "The power to tax is the power to destroy." The Founding Fathers of this nation believed the taxing powers should be reserved for the states and local governments. Madison warned future generations that if the American people began to advocate taxation from the central government this nation would head into trouble. This goes against the nature of things. These men understood the dangers of taxing because of the way England had burdened them with unnecessary taxes. They believed that taxing from the central system was to be avoided and reserved solely for local and state governments.

"Well, how are we going to pay for services then?" one may ask. Simple, but not a very good question if one was familiar with the real intent of the U.S. Constitution.

Well, there are some democrats whom I admire and support. Thomas Jefferson is one first and foremost. There is a former governor of Alaska who, if he were to run in an election today, I would probably attempt to vote him back into office. It would really depend on what kind of republican who ran against him. I supported his efforts to cut down the bureaucracy, trim the budget, and make government more responsible to the people. This concept is as old as the idea that man naturally craves the ability to govern himself. If a moderate republican were to run against a conservative democrat with these beliefs, I may be inclined to vote for the latter.

We need to be mindful of a group of both democrats and republicans who dub themselves as progressives. The progressive movement is designed to take away our natural right to govern ourselves. The purpose of this movement is to take over every aspect of government and make people more and more dependent upon their false kindness and heeding. The progressive movement began nearly a hundred years ago, and worked underground, so to speak, until the right time came. Their purpose is to take control of every aspect of government and eventually convert our system into socialism. We have a growing number of people coming out of the woodwork as we speak, and they are gaining momentum every day.

The problem, I believe, the elder George Bush had in the last election was that he lost sight of the focus of the Republican Party. He became, in my opinion, more concerned about the party rather than focusing on the philosophy of less government, balancing the budget, real family values, hard work, erosion of freedoms, etc. I'm sorry, but in my opinion, George Bush didn't live up to his predecessor's reputation. He could have if he had not lost his focus because he had an excellent teacher.

I, like Ronald Reagan, was a democrat first. Reagan broke away from that party because the people affiliated with the faction became more party orientated than people orientated. This group was committed to staying close to the working class. Instead it began to respond more and more to the social quandaries. In time it advocated more and more social programs, and to pay for these services, the party had to advocate more and more taxes. So, Reagan broke away and became one of the most dedicated and renowned republicans in American history. During the last Presidential Election there wasn't a democratic candidate running whom I supported, and I had trouble making up my mind about the republican candidates. There was one guy I liked, but he was so far down in the polls that it would have been a miracle for him to have made a respectable showing. So, I just sat back and waited for a spell.

Well—that was my privilege, wasn't it?

I hope my mother won't hold that against me.

Now let me conclude with these notes: I love the constitution which formed our government because it is the most correct governmental document, in its original form, that has ever been introduced throughout the recorded history of the human race; it is the most inspired instrument about how governments should be conducted and the concepts are based upon the natural, God-given rights that every government should guarantee to all mankind.

I am pro-liberty, pro-freedom and self-government, pro-independence, pro SOVEREIGNTY, and pro-everything that has made our country the greatest nation ever on the face of the earth.

I am anti-socialist, anti-welfare state, anti-communist, and anti-everything which would deprive me of my life, my liberty and ownership of property and, of course, my own pursuit of happiness.

Well, I guess I'm just a red-blooded, old fashioned, proud American.

And an Alaskan Native one at that.

U.S. FOREST SERVICE SETS THE PACE

June 22, 1995

One evening in 1993 I received a call from a board member of the Yakutat Native Association. The President of the board had resigned and they wanted someone to fill the vacant seat. She asked me if I would like to fill the seat until the next election. My immediate response was "No thanks."

An hour later I received another call. "Bert, we really need someone to fill this seat, and your name keeps popping up—how about it?"

"No thanks," I said. At this time, I was busy working on some articles for the Tundra Times and polishing some short stories to submit to the Alaska Native Magazine. I really wasn't prepared to take on any other responsibilities at the time.

"Oh, well, okay," she said, and we hung up.

About 11:30 P.M., there was another phone call. I had been in slumber land for a couple hours already. "Bert," she said. "Your name keeps coming up in our discussions. Here's what we are proposing to you. Why don't you just accept our offer to fill this seat until the next election? This will only be an eight-month appointment and someone else will be elected at that time."

There was a long silence before I answered. "Eight months, huh?"

"Yes—eight months, and you'll be free to do what you want."

There was another long silence—. Eight months, I said to myself, isn't long.

"Are you still there, Bert?"

"Yep, I'm still here."

"How does that sound to you?"

"Well—it sounds okay—but—"

"Eight months only, and you'll be free to write your books and articles...."

"Okay," I gave in. "When do you want me to start?"

"Could you come down now and we'll accept your appointment and swear you in."

"Why—it's almost midnight!" I exclaimed.

"This will only take a few minutes."

I walked into the room to find four tired, beaming, women waiting for me. To make the appointment legal I was asked to write a short note expressing my interest in the position. Someone made a motion and it was seconded to accept me as a member of the Yakutat Native Association Board of Directors.

They decided that they were going to reorganize the board since they didn't have a President. They elected me President. It happened so fast that, as a first, new, member I didn't even have a chance to vote yea or nay on the issue,

There was a Self-Governance Demonstration Conference forthcoming in Washington, DC in two weeks, and so they said that a good way for me to get familiar with tribal government they voted to authorize me to attend the meeting.

The evening of the first day of the conference there was a United States Department of Agriculture (USDA) meeting held in the same hotel, and I was encouraged by some new acquaintances to listen to a tribal leader, Chief William Burke of the Confederated Tribes of the Umatilla Reservation, deliver the key-note address. I was thrilled about the message that was given that evening. Chief Burke changed my whole outlook on the power of tribes and their potential for determining our future.

"There are three sovereigns in the Government to Government relationship," he began with his opening statement. "These sovereigns," he pointed out, "are Tribes, States, and the U.S. Government."

On April 29, 1994, I attended another meeting where President Bill Clinton invited elected tribal leaders to the White House where he signed the American Indian/Alaska Native Policy MEMORANDUM FOR THE HEADS OF EXECUTIVE DEPARTMENTS AND AGENCIES; this directive required that all federal agencies were to begin working with Native American Tribal Governments on a <u>real</u> government-to-government relationship.

The seed of this directive was generated as a result of the self-governance concept, a tribally driven initiative which sprung from tribal leaders spanning from "sea to shining sea" of America. This initiative became a demonstration project by act of Congress where seven tribes were allowed to test the model. Each year a group of tribes were accepted into the compact and in 1994 the legislation became permanent at which time twenty-nine tribes were added into the pact. This concept reminded me about one of our unalienable rights mentioned in the Constitution which implores that we have the right to self-government. This idea also comes from the Natural Law.

The BIA, as we speak, has begun the process of downsizing and restructuring. In 1994 the Indian Health Service interred into a self-governance demonstration project and is, with budget cuts and restraints, experiencing downsizing, yet attempting to structure their services to provide more with less funding.

As an aside from President Clinton's invitation to D.C. in the spring of 1994 a group of powerful tribal leaders had a one-day meeting to discuss ways on how the new functions of the BIA could be applied to other federal agencies. Guiding principles from the meeting was submitted to the Department of Interior. Because of our brainstorming Ada Deer, Assistant Secretary of Interior, made the Non-BIA announcement in the fall of 1994. What this meant was tribes would be able to assume functions, programs, services or activities from agencies within Department of Interior which have cultural, historical or geographical significance to tribes in Indian Country. As an example, some tribes are eyeing fish hatcheries which are administered under the U.S. Fish and Wildlife Service. This new directive allowed tribal governments to actually take over management of that program. Under President Clinton's directive, that government agency would begin the process of interring into an Annual Funding Agreement (AFA) with the tribe to assume that particular program. This would bring the program, service, function, or activity to the local level and provide jobs for qualified tribal members. "Even though this might be hypothetical it can become real, and will, when tribes catch the full vision of how they can implement this concept," says Danny Jordon from the Hoopa Valley Tribe in California.

Even though these programs fall within the Department of Interior and the Indian Health Service is in the Department of Health and Human Services, the U.S. Forest Service has taken a pro-active stance and has been working toward developing a better relationship with Tribal Governments. The odd thing about this is that the Forest Service is under the Department of Agriculture and so is not obliged to follow the Non-BIA prerequisites mandated like the Department of Interior.

In March of 1995 the Forest Service made available to their staff a working draft titled the Forest Service National Resource Book on American Indian and Alaska Native Relationship.

"The Forest Service is really working hard to try and work with tribal governments," said Gill Truitt, a tribal council member from the Sitka Tribes of Alaska. Sitka Tribes is one the first of southeast Alaska tribes to inter into a Memorandum of Understanding (MOU) with the Forest Service. Hoonah Indian Association has had an MOU since 1993. "We've been having regular meetings with the Forest Service," says Tribal President Kenneth Grant. "These meetings eliminate a lot of bad rumors. I feel they are making a good faith effort," he adds. The Yakutat Native Association was organized as a tribal non-profit and the village of Yakutat accepted the federally recognized tribal status and thus became the Yakutat Tlingit Tribe in 1994. It now has an MOU with the Forest Service. As we speak the Angoon IRA is in the process of signing an MOU as well.

"However, if Congress passes the Tongass Reform and the Landless Bills," Kenneth Grant observes, "it might change things because it will open up the Lug II lands for logging activities." Lug II lands are section of lands in the Tongass National Forest Plan that have been designated for no logging or any kind of commercial development.

Yakutat provides, in their MOU, a provision for the protection of Lug II lands for any type of adverse development, particularly logging. Monti Fujishin, from the Yakutat Ranger office thinks Yakutat is doing well based on numerous "situations of relationship with the tribe the past couple of years. If we are going to survive in the next five or ten years," he observes, "we have to develop a lot of partnerships. The Cultural Heritage Plan is a good example." He was referring to the Cultural Heritage Plan the Yakutat Tlingit Tribe completed with a National Parks Service Grant later this year. This involved the participation of government agencies and organizations in the community of Yakutat. Fujishin emphasized that this is the kind of cooperation the community of Yakutat needs to continue if the community expects positive things to happen.

The Forest Service's Hand Book recognizes that there is a government-to-government relationship with federally recognized tribes. The MOU that President Clinton signed also states that the federal government should assess the impact of federal regulations, projects, programs, activities and services about trust responsibilities and assure that tribal government rights are considered. It also says that federal agencies should remove any procedural impediments so that tribes can function in a positive way as well as develop their regions economically. Mr. Clinton's statement says that executive departments and agencies "will work cooperatively with other federal departments and support cooperative efforts with tribal governments."

Even though tribe's relationship is primarily with the federal government, the state governments cannot be ignored. The State of Alaska has had a problem in the past with recognizing tribal governments in Alaska. The Associated Press announced in the Anchorage Daily News on November 17, 1995 that the State of Alaska concedes Native Tribal status, which now opens the door very wide for tribes to begin appealing to the Knowles Administration with the spirit of the self-governance concept.

Chief William Burke also completed his statement by saying, "Those three sovereigns" (meaning the Tribes, States, and U.S. Governments) "need to work together to solve problems with three principles—Honesty, Open-mindedness and Willingness."

Many tribal leaders feel confident that the U.S. Forest Service is making an honest effort which should set the pace for other federal agencies, particularly the State of Alaska, with this endeavor of self-governance for Alaska Natives and rural villages.

MANY SOLUTIONS FOUND WITHIN OUR CONSTITUTION

December 20, 1994

As Native Americans the tribulations we cope with on a daily bases are, no doubt, thought-provoking and challenging ones. However, as I have demonstrated in other articles, the dilemmas we tolerate are not only confined to our Native communities. They are not just ours and ours alone; they are widespread problems and belong to other people as well. Therefore we, as Americans, have a duty to keep and place run-a-way events in natural order.

When we embark upon the task of solving our problems, history has invariably proven that it is wisest to understand what the root of problems are. History has also proven that, in many of our quandaries, we have a tendency to try to mend things with band aids—but these repairs have always been verified as temporary ones. A good example is when the federal government passes continuing resolutions to keep the government working instead of passing a budget. Again, isn't it much better to get to the root of problems rather than these afflictions invariably come to us in the form of political, economic, and social issues—and as a result we appeal to government to solve these ills?

Will Durant, in his books about the stories of civilization, frequently made a point that one of the downfalls of civilizations was the breakdown of the family unit. The progressives in our society today are laboring diligently to interfere with good old family values. I will not blame the following story on the progressives; however, the federal government and Christian missionaries were responsible for the ways our traditional Tlingit culture was altered.

In the olden days Tlingit children were given to their uncles and aunts when seven or eight years old for proper training on how to survive in the wilderness and how to gather and prepare foods. The reason for this transformation was because natural parents lacked the fortitude to discipline their children. Young men learned from their uncles how to live within the circle of the Natural Law; thereby they were adequately equipped to provide resources for a village's survival. When the federal and religious entities removed this element of survival from our culture, the so-called apple cart was dramatically upset. Many children from my generation were educated in boarding schools because our villages did not have high schools in those days. In this new and strange environment, we were lacking the importance of family relationships. When we graduated from high school and got married and began to raise our own families, and when we began to have high schools in our villages, many from this generation had embedded in their habits that the schools should do everything for our children. It was a disappointing change for young adults when they returned to their villages lacking parental guidance when they began having their own families. A generation and a half or two have been recovering from this culture clash and struggling to find their way even to this day.

Now when we discuss family relationship, I believe we would endorse a father, mother and children. To expand this nice little circle, we must include grandparents and other extended family members; uncles and aunts play only a minor role these days— mostly supportive in nature. In modern day culture the core of the family unit is incomplete when either one of the parents are absent. State regulations mandates that it is really the responsibility of parents to teach their children proper values. I firmly believe that our schools should prepare our children to learn how to earn a living, while it is the duty of the home to teach one how to live a life. Additionally, religious institutions and other organizations such as schools are only helpers to the home.

I strongly believe that the lessons of teaching proper values are not the role of schools, yet many people from my culture have come to believe this. To emphasize the importance of parental responsibility I will cite this example:

Several years ago, I was watching 60 Minutes, a popular CBS television news magazine. Near the end of the program Andy Rooney was given a few minutes to comment on any issue that strikes his fancy. This commentary was on the family. He essentially said that "if we want to have good children we are going to have to raise good parents." What a timely statement!

Not only is it timely but it is true for all people in this day and age. The proper role of government, on the other hand, is conclusively stated in the Declaration of Independence. Government was instituted for the purpose of controlling the conduct of people, while constitutions were designed to control the conduct of government. The purpose of governments, then, is to protect us—to protect our lives, our liberties, and to guarantee us our pursuit of happiness and the family unit is, of course, the source of where one can achieve happiness. I don't think that it is within the role of government to dictate how our families should be raised. Religious training, on the other hand, can help parents teach their children how to live a life and should have the freedom to do so.

Thomas Jefferson believed that our system of government was designed to keep the government in check and the Constitution is supposed is to keep the government from getting into mischief. It tells our President, our legislature and our courts what they can and cannot do. Yet, there are a couple of amendments to the Constitution that has become detrimental to our health and welfare. One has to do with the erosion of state's rights.

The 17th Amendment to the Constitution crippled the proper power of the legislature by doing away with the appointment of the senators by the respective state legislatures and made senators an elective position by the people. Before, senators were obligated to look after the best interest of their respective states, while those who live in the House of

Representatives were elected by the people and were obligated to look after the best interest of the people.

Every American, Native and non-native alike, should embark upon a serious study of our U.S. Constitution and learn, for themselves, what the framers really intended. As we do this we will get a better perspective of what it is that governments should do for us.

Now what can we, as common American citizens, do to bring our people in government, and the government, back to their proper roles?

Most of all we must build strong families. This means that fathers and mothers should be married, and children taught how to live a life.

We must see that the legislatures will have to begin making laws based on commons sense, rather than listening to the special interest groups and lobbyists.

We must be watchful that the President carry-out the laws, rather than creating legislation through his executive orders and proclamations.

We must keep a scrutinizing eye on the Supreme Court and see that they interpret the Constitution and avoid the danger of making legislation through its written decisions.

The federal government is going to have to stop interfering with state's rights and let the states and local government serve their citizens. The only time the federal government should interfere is when matters involve issues on a national scale. State and local governments can better serve its citizens from the local level.

To help cut our national debt and balance the federal budget, we are going to have to learn what the real intent of the "Promote the general welfare" and the "Interstate Commerce "clauses in the Constitution really means. The Founding Fathers bitterly debated these clauses before they included them in the Constitution, and then cautioned future generations about the dangers of misinterpretation. These warnings can be found in the Federalist Papers and every high school and college curricula should make these required reading in their civic classes.

Another damaging amendment to the Constitution was the 16th Amendment. In the original Constitution, the power to tax was reserved for states and then the states were obliged to contribute into the federal treasury according to that state's population to handle issues and problems on a national scale, such as road building between states or on the national defense.

We, indeed, live in a country that is blessed. No other nation has risen to such proportions as the United States in such a short period of time—that was because of the way our Constitution was framed, which indicates to us how government should operate with its checks and balances be honored.

We, as Alaska Natives, fought long and hard to be recognized as citizens. I think we can adequately and rightfully so, pen a phrase from the Declaration of Independence stated in the final paragraph: "—we mutually pledge to each other our lives, our fortunes, and our sacred honor."

Our forefathers, indeed, accomplished that through blood, sweat and tears. We have the Alaska Native Brotherhood Constitution to thank for that. I liken the Alaska. Native Brotherhood Constitution to the U.S. Constitution in its original form. Article I say that Native people will participate in the civil government from the local, state and national levels under the spirit of the "Declaration of Independence and the Constitution and laws of the United States."

The way we can attain happiness, which is one of the reasons why our government was set up, is to participate in government. Our task is to learn all we can about constitutional government and what the real intent of the Founding Fathers was, and then make our contribution to righting wrongs committed against us as citizens based on the principles of love of God, country and family, and the Natural Law. We are, indeed, supposed to be the watch-dog of government; we shouldn't let government do what we, ourselves, could be thrown in jail for. When we begin to keep government in check and balanced we will set the stage for helping other people to do the same as well.

Keeping balance means abiding by the Natural Law.

The Declaration of Independence clearly states that when our government(s) no longer accomplishes those ends then we are obligated to abolish or alter that government and start a new one based on those same principles[36]—that is the protection of our lives, liberties and properties. We can do a lot toward bringing our country back on the right track again by insisting that governments—national, state, tribal and local, be put back in their proper constitutional order.

Yes, as Native Americans, we have a lot of problems—but again those problems are not so unusual that they are confined just to our Native communities. They are the same problems other ethnic groups and people of the United States are facing, and when we gather, as true Americans, and identify with these issues together, then we can begin to fittingly solve the social ills of our nation as well.

Living according to the Law of Nature and Nature's God will surely help us live in friendship of those values.

---

[36] The Declaration of Independence

ARE WE A DEMOCRACY OR A REPUBLIC?

Saturday, February 29, 2004

A couple weeks ago I was flying home from Anchorage, Alaska and I overheard someone in the seat behind me explaining the difference between a democracy and a republic to a friend. I was very enlightened with his understanding of how government should function in our American society.

"Okay," he said. "When we place our hand across our heart and recite the Pledge of Allegiance and we come to that part 'and to the _____ for which it stands,' what do we say?"

After a long pause, the reply came back. "Why it's obvious the answer is a republic."

So, what are a democracy and a republic?

Many people I have talked to agree that the Founding Fathers of this nation were very wise and, if anything else, extremely clever. Having gone through the experience of building this new nation they, indeed, had an appreciation of great nations that have come and gone, not to mention the fact that they had been dealing with a king who had practically done everything bad that a bad king could do to his subjects.

The Framers instituted a limited form of government because they foresaw the dangers of a central government with absolute power. They also saw the dangers of a democracy, which philosophy delegated absolute power to most of the people. So, the signers of the Constitution were out-rightly opposed to a pure democracy, therefore the system which they brain stormed was in no way a democracy. What it really boiled down to was that we ended up with a republic.

The Founding Fathers had preference over a republic as opposed to a democracy. Not only did the so-called republic designate a limited form of central government, but its philosophy provided that the people would elect the best men from among themselves and then delegate to these people the administration of the affairs of government. In actuality, what they were doing was allowing a few good men to do what many good men could not do for themselves as individuals. With this kind of system government could be held in check when people elected to the various offices tended to become unscrupulous; then citizens still had enough control to make sure that once reliable characters, who became capricious for some reason, had a chance to mend their ways, or be replaced at the next election. See, the Constitution does provide for term limitations. And it was left to the people to decide how long an incumbent should last.

If things got really bad then there were recall and impeachment provisions spelled out in the Constitution, which is supposed to be the last resort technique to get undesirable men out of office. This, in another sense, is representative government, and it falls under the identity of a republic.

One serious aspect of subjecting ourselves under the philosophy of a republic was that it could not succeed if dishonest, unethical, and cunning folk were elected into government.

One serious concern we should consider is that we ought not to let government do what we would be thrown in jail for. Congress, for instance, several years ago experienced a myriad of congressmen abusing their check writing privileges from the congressional bank. As an individual I would be (and have been) penalized by my banker, or the person with whom the bad check was written can prosecute, and I would not only have to make the check good but would be fined and may even serve a jail sentence. But certain congressmen were able to get away with bad check writing.

And—what about whitewater? We still haven't heard the whole story about that yet; however, during the presidential campaign the candidate's womanizing was quickly swept under the carpet. The issue here is not whether the candidate will be able to carry out what he promised—it is his character that is at stake.

Gary Hart wasn't so lucky.

And what about our own Alaskan Native State legislature who was accused of sexual harassment? If he had been known as a man of good character he would not have gotten himself in such a predicament in the first place. These kinds of chaps are hard to get out of office because of the way they are.

And so, as the Framers deliberated considerably about whether they should form a government on the principles of a democracy they realized, of course, that an absolute democracy could lead to an unlimited administration of government.

And then there was this republic idea. A republic is a limited, representative type of government. The extreme to this philosophy is "no government" or the less government we have the better off we will be to pursue happiness.[37] The Founders realized that this type of control is no control at all.

So, the Founders said, "Let's create a republican form government and insert it in Article IV, Section 4 so we wouldn't forget." What I believe that people have been doing of late is forgetting to read and understand the Constitution. The real purpose for embracing this type of body politic was to bring the two philosophies toward the middle—in the direction of people's law. From the democratic (liberal) side of the spectrum, the people would elect their representatives and let government attempt to solve our problems; from the republic (conservative) idea they would be represented by politicians who would strive to keep the government on a limited plain.[38]

There were times when we witnessed this happen? Let's see, invariably over the years we normally see one party control congress

---

[37] See Spectrum Of The Constitutional Eagle
[38] Abid

and the opposite in the executive branch or vice versa. We hear people call this gridlock. We hear folks exclaim, "let's get those liberals (or conservatives) out of there so things can get things done!" And we hear others proclaim, "Let's take back America and replace that president!"

Another issue we need to consider is the importance of the Native vote and that of voting for candidate's that will benefit the Native people. It is true the Native vote is critical—but so is everyone else's.[39] What we as Alaskans and Americans need to do is become familiar with the concept of constitutional government and what government is supposed to do for us— and when we go to the poles we should vote for what is good for America rather than caving into special interest groups.

Let's take the Declaration of Independence for instance. It states that the purpose for forming this republic was to guarantee to all the protection of our lives, our liberties and our pursuit of happiness. And so, from that concept our republic was formed, and the Constitution was designed to keep government in check and the government was supposed to control the conduct of people. The Constitution, in its original form, did not authorize the government to take care of us—the intent was for government to protect us and promote the free enterprise system which purpose was to manage the economy.

So, before we go to the poles to cast our ballots we should know who your candidates are and what they stand for. And they shouldn't be catering to get the Native vote because of what they can and will promise us. The real question they ought to know is what should government do for us as Alaskans, and on a larger scale, as Americans?

---

[39] I was dismayed during the last primary election when Joe Miller defeated incumbent Lisa Murkowski for one of Alaska's senate seats. Senator Murkowski, at the urging of the Native people of Alaska, decided to run as a "write-in" candidate. There were some important issues in Congress that Native people were concerned about. One was the so-called "over selection" of lands held back as a result of the Alaska Native Land Claims Settlement Act; Senator Murkowski was in the process of accelerating the land transfer through Congress. And, of course, all the pork that former senator Ted Stevens was able to bring to rural Alaska was on the agenda as well.

We, the people, are, of course, the watch guard of our rights as citizens, and we elect, supposedly, highly motivated statesmen to represent us who are committed to preserving our lives, our liberties and guaranteeing us our pursuit of happiness.

Of course, if we are not highly ethical ourselves, it would be a nonplus to elect dishonest men and women to office. That of fostering an honest society is a must if a republican form of government is going to flourish.

Alexis de Tocqueville was a French historian and political scientist who made an eighteen-month tour through the United States in the mid 1800's. He was sent by his government to find out why America became such a great nation in such a short period of time. He found his answer when he went into the churches throughout the country. As a result of his findings he wrote a two-volume book entitled *DEMOCRACY IN AMERICA*. One interesting statement he made was this: ***"Religion in America takes no direct part in the government of society, but it must be regarded as the first of their political institutions—"*** In another part he said that ***"America is great because America is good. America will cease to be great only when it ceases to be good."*** Herein lays the root of Native American problems. Herein lays the root of America's dire ills.

Well, when we learn what it means to be a republic we come to understand that a republic is a lot different than our concept of what a democracy is.

It is a republic which the Founding Fathers of this nation established as the form of government for which we should live. A limited, representative form of government was the most desirable, and it requires a highly moral people to flourish in this kind of society.

This is the kind of society we should all be striving for.

Well we may admit that the Founders were very wise and clever. They risked their lives, their fortunes and their sacred honor by placing their faith in the future of the American people.

So, the next time we place our hands across our heart and say in unison, "I pledge allegiance to the flag and to the United States of

America and to the—" we don't say "democracy for which it stands—." We, of course say, "Republic."

When I was gathering my stuff to de-plane in Yakutat, I turned to my anonymous stranger, gave him my two thumbs up and said, "Right on."

IMPROPER ROLE OF GOVERNMENT

When the Framers brought forth the U.S. Constitution their intent regarding the proper role of government is certainly a far cry different from what the American people are requiring from our federal system in this day and age. To aid us in engineering everything into focus it is necessary for Americans to seriously study this instrument; the purpose should be to discover how the Constitution was designed to help government serve the people. As we do this we will understand how we, as Native Americans, fit into the general scheme of things. Possibly, then, our federal, state, local and tribal governments will fall into proper perspective. In this work we will examine government's role; in particular we will investigate whether the Framers intended that government should provide for economic growth and jobs. Does the federal government have the right to regulate how the economy should function? To find an answer it is necessary to learn what the Framers of the Constitution had in mind regarding the free enterprise system as well as the "Promote the General Welfare" clause in the Preamble and the "Interstate Commerce" clause in the Constitution.

The Constitution was brought forth to carry out what the Declaration of Independence pronounced—that is to come forth with a basic set of regulations that would protect our lives, our liberties and properties, and to ensure that every American under the protection of this country could enjoy the freedom to obtain happiness. So, a government was formed through the Constitution for the purpose of controlling the conduct of people, and the Constitution was going to be responsible for controlling the conduct of government.

It is important to note this because the Constitution was brought forth for the purpose of limiting the central government, so the free enterprise system can provide for the economic stability in the lives of the public. The free enterprise system caused some interesting debates among the Founding Fathers, but when it came down to the truth it was agreed that the free market would be the best system for economic growth for America. Because it fostered competition among the private sector, Americans were able to get the better deal much cheaper and more efficient than the way government could. It is because of the free enterprise system that America became an economic power. America became powerful because people prospered. People prospered because of private enterprise. Then why isn't the free enterprise system working today? The reason is government could not keep its nose out of the business of free industry in this country; another reason is, because it is human nature, that when people realize what a good thing they have greed takes over honorable practices.

The "promote the general welfare" clause is the most misunderstood clause in the Constitution. Note that it says promote not provide. The real intent of the Framers was that monies appropriated by Congress were to be spent for the <u>welfare for the whole country</u>, not for special interest groups. James Madison, one of the Framers and co-author of the Federalist Papers echoed a warning:

"If Congress can employ money indefinitely for the general welfare, and are the sole and supreme judges of the general welfare, they may take the care of religion into their own hands; they may appoint teachers in every state, county and parish and pay them out of the public treasury, they may take into their own hands the education of children, the establishing in like manner schools throughout the union; <u>they may assume the provision of the poor</u>..."

The Constitution does not empower the government the authority to spend on these types of social issues. Today when Congress is debating the mandate of the mid-term elections about cutting spending, they seem to target social security and Medicare and make no mention of entitlements that really are robbing the tax box—such as food stamps and general assistance programs that make people more dependent rather than self-sufficient. When we come to understand a little about government spending we must realize that it is also given the power to tax "to pay the debts and provide for the common defense and general welfare of the United States." No one should have any problem about paying debts for the "common defense," however there is some misunderstanding about how the government should spend for the "general welfare."

Thomas Jefferson believed that this clause did not give the power to tax for the general welfare of the people—the real intent was to limit the power of taxation from the federal level for the general welfare of "the union" or the federal government. There is a difference between a grant of positive power to tax and a restriction on the power to tax. The real intent of the Founders of the U.S. Constitution regarding the welfare clause was that government should promote and encourage the general welfare, not provide for it. It is the free enterprise system that will provide for the general welfare by creating a healthy economy—a vigorous economy creates jobs. The more people who are working in the private sector the more tax dollars will be filtered into the federal treasury.

Another clause in the Constitution considered to be very important is the so-called "Commerce Clause." It says: "The Congress shall have power...to regulate commerce with foreign nations and, among the several states, and with the Indian tribes." In the beginning the emphasis was on commerce rather than regulation. The keystone to national unity was the free flow of commerce between the states, and then to promote commerce between nations. Over a period of time there was the gradual expansion of federal regulations over every aspect of the interstate and international commerce. The free enterprise system should work between states and nations as well—but it isn't working because the federal government has seen fit to put restrictions on the free flow of market. With the health care bill passed proponents of the massive taxing power proclaimed that they could use the commerce clause. Now folks, isn't this the reverse of what the Constitution, in its original form, dictates? Isn't the Constitution the one that's supposed to limit government?

Regarding the federal government's power to regulate commerce with the various Indians tribes—the only area in which the commerce clause was used in commercial activities among the Indians has been in connection with the sale of alcohol to them.

Governments cannot create jobs. The only way jobs can be created is through a healthy economy. A healthy economy is stimulated by competition between private enterprise—by the free flow of trade between private companies among the various states and nations. Realize this, when NAFCA was passed by congress America got back into compliance with the Constitution.

The Constitution, in its original form, did not authorize the federal government to interfere with private enterprise, nor did it authorize the federal government to compete with private businesses. Yet today, the federal government is involved in the regulation of business and is in direct competition with the free flow of trade and commerce—and it is our tax monies the government is using to accomplish these ends.

When we complain about how high our taxes are considering the fact that the federal government ought to stop competing with private enterprise and go back to the principles of protecting our lives, our liberties and our properties. Maybe we ought to remember that our federal government should to go back to the idea of encouraging the true intent of the "General Welfare" and "Interstate Commerce" clauses and get out of the business of competing with business.

When politicians tell you that their economic program is better than the other because their theory will create more jobs, we have every right to become suspicious.

Governments can't create jobs.

Only enterprising people and the free enterprise system can.

TEN CENTS ON THE DOLLAR

Sunday, June 15, 2003

"How much do I owe you, John, for this fine haircut?" the young soldier asked.

"Ten cents for the haircut and ninety cents tax," was my dad's reply.

Little did people, of that time, realize what a prophetic statement was made by my father's witty reply.

During the Second World War, Yakutat had the largest military airbase in Alaska with up to 15,000 troops. Our little community of no more than 300 souls was a place I remember full of activity, not only with the everyday hustle and bustle of folks who carved a living from the commercial fishing ventures, but with friendships I remember my parents and people of the village had fondly established with many of the young men who had volunteered a short period of their lives to the ideals and freedoms upon which this country was founded.

My father was what he called a "cat skinner" which translates to a heavy equipment operator, or more specifically a caterpillar operator. Every time I take off the runways or land in Yakutat on Alaska Airlines, I am reminded about how his co-workers had nicknamed him "Muskeg" because he, at the beginning of the construction of the runways, was operating his cat digging and moving dirt and swampy material, creating a huge ditch that would eventually be filled with rock, sand and gravel in preparation for the asphalt surfacing.

Now I'm not sure how my dad became a heavy equipment operator, but I know from hearings stories by those who knew him that he was a good one. Nor do I know how he became a barber; I do know that he was a good one because he had cut my brother and my hair many a time.

I do remember, however, that he started with those ancient, now antique, hand clippers. My dad became a very popular barber during those days. With the military he would go on base and cut the GI's hair every Saturday and it was then that he inherited from his army buddies an electric hair cutter. When the war ended, and the military moved out the Army gave him the barber chair that he used when he was cutting hair on base. From that time on, every Saturday mornings, he would move that chair from the corner of the room in our house and put it in the middle of the room. And then he would hang his barber shop shingle outside his door which read:

Haircuts 10 cents

Tax: 90 cents

If this were real, he would have been paying 90% of his one dollar he made from each haircut into the government's coffer; 10% would be his to add to his own treasury.

In reality as well, this is the direction our hard-earned dollars, through the federal graduated income tax, is routing very quickly. That's why, in my April 2002 column I wrote how the "Founding Father's" (by the way, I understand there's a movement not to use this term any more) believed that the power to tax by the federal system was the power to destroy the soul of America[40]. What they feared was if the central government was given the authority to tax on our incomes that America would, over a period of several decades, become impoverished. And the reason we would become insolvent was because "big brother" would begin this process of redistributing wealth without any effort on the part of the recipients. Let me say that in this day and age there are two factions of people in America: the givers and the takers. Very rapidly the takers are outnumbering the givers, and this is one other reason why America is in financial discord. Last month my article addressed why

---

[40] See Power To Tax The Power To Destroy

the U.S. Constitution reserved the taxing powers to states and local governments.[41]

One of the most damaging amendments to the U.S. Constitution was the 16th one. We should abolish it and bring the taxing powers back where it belongs. When this happens then you'll see local governments begin to prosper, likewise the state governments will have more control over their fiscal affairs, and the federal system will be brought to its proper size.

---

[41] See States Should Have Taxing Powers

ABSOLUTE POWER TO TAX SHOULD BE A STATE RIGHT

Monday, May 19, 2003

Some time ago I said to myself, "Oh, oh," when I learned some states weren't generating an adequate amount of revenue.[42] The federal government was eliminating funding to states and the cuts adversely affected the state's ability to provide essential services they had become accustomed to from the federal coffers. In the news lately, there were concerns that these cuts will prompt states to increase taxes to meet their budget obligations.

When the Sixteenth Amendment to the U.S. Constitution was ratified this empowered the central government to impose a direct tax on our incomes. This adjustment in the way the federal government could tax caused a passionate debate on the floors of Congress; however, it really boiled down to a contest between some smart-alec Democrats and Republicans.

In 1909 Senator Bailey, a Democrat from Texas, introduced an Amendment to a tariff bill. When it looked like the motion was going to pass the Republicans introduced an income tax bill as an amendment to the Constitution. The Republicans voted for the Amendment because they felt that it would sidetrack attention from the Bailey Bill. Well,

---

[42] As we speak many states are experiencing lack of funding to keep their budgets balanced; even so many major cities are on the brink of bankruptcy

we all know what it takes to pass a Constitutional amendment: must be passed by both houses and then ratified by two thirds of the states. The Republicans felt that the amendment idea was going to be defeated, thereby ending the debate on this issue of an income tax. The Democrats felt compelled to vote on the bill because it was their initiative and they didn't want to see the Republicans take the credit. The House approved it by a vote of 318 to 14 and the Senate passed it 77 to zip.[43]

Congressman S.E. Payne of New York admitted that the purpose for his vote was to defeat the Bailey Bill and that most of the Congress, in reality, did not want an income tax. Here is what the Constitutional textbook says: "Contrary to all expectation, the Income Tax Amendment was ratified by one State Legislature after another and was proclaimed in effect on February 25, 1913."[44] Shame on the American people of that day! They should have known better—particularly about our history—

The Founders, during their debates in Constitutional Hall, consummated in Article I, Section 9, Clause 4 a provision that direct income taxes must be apportioned to the States according to population. In other words, States were given the absolute power to tax, and then they would contribute to the federal treasurer according to the strength of its taxing powers by the number of people in the state. This ability also trickled to local governments so taxing powers was really reserved for state and local governments.

One reason the Founders wanted the federal government to stay out of the taxing business was that they knew what would happen once the American people realized what this method could do. Their concern was that it would stifle the spirituality, the self-sufficient mind-set of the American people, as well as their temporal well-being.

Congressman Payne commented on the amendment by saying: "It is a tax on the rascals— "and "—one that makes a nation of liars."[45] I think what he meant by this is that when the central government taxes people's incomes to redistribute the wealth this would cause people to

---

[43] Writings of W. Cleon Skousen
[44] Abide
[45] Abide

bicker over the funds for their own special interests. We see a lot of that happening today, don't we?

The U.S. Constitution guarantees the American people a Republican form of government. No—it is not the political party we know; it is a form of government that is limited in its powers. I believe the Founders wanted the taxing powers of the central government to be small in nature so that states and local governments can better serve their people more effectively and efficiently by using their taxing abilities.

In my February column of 2002 I talked about the immoral act of the federal government imposing taxes on our direct incomes. The Power to Tax, The Power to Destroy is worth thought-provoking study, serious public debate and critical pondering upon.

LET'S REFLECT UPON OUR TAXING HISTORY

After reading one of my latest articles, a longtime friend asked me, "Do you really believe that local and state governments should have the absolute power to tax?" My reply was "Absolutely." Perhaps now is an opportune time to re-learn how the Founders structured the way governments should behave as well as flourish.

I have made myself clear in previous commentaries that the Founders of this country had impeccable vision. Recently there has been a lot of discussion about a myriad of taxes aimed at bridging the states' fiscal gap. We have heard about raids on the Permanent Fund in Alaska to imposing an income tax, and even implementing a statewide and national sales tax. These hair brained ideas clearly go along with the Founder's warnings that the power to tax is the power to destroy if we fail in this challenge to properly use taxing powers. Now may be a good time to bring common sense back into the American lifeblood. Let's start by learning what the Founders said about this issue of taxation with (or without) representation.

They adamantly warned the central government to steer clear of the taxing business. Article I, Section 2, paragraph 3 of the U.S. Constitution states that direct taxes shall be apportioned among the states according to that states' population. They realized that state and local governments would be able to subsist effectively by allowing the people to thrive off the resources in their respective areas and provide essential services by the appropriate ability to tax. It was believed that states should have the capability to tax on our direct incomes, while the municipalities would utilize the sales and property taxes. When individuals prosper, they will make their contribution thereby avoid imposing unnecessary burdens in their pocket books. Then the states would contribute to the federal coffers, so the central government could meet its essential obligations such as providing for the common defense and promoting the general welfare of the American people. You see, the Founders were trying to help us avoid what the Mother Country had overburdened them with. Unfortunately, when the progressive movement began the Sixteenth Amendment changed that concept and gave the federal system the absolute power to tax on our incomes; over a period of more than half a century the federal government has grown to such large proportions that it has taken over nearly every part of our lives!

America is a rich country—we have an abundance of resources that we can, collectively, feed the whole world. Alaska, likewise, is blessed with natural resources we can all benefit from. But consider this, if you will—the federal government claims it owns 66% of Alaska, the state has control over about 28% and corporations (private sector) have the rest. Did you know that the U.S. Constitution did not allow the central government to own land? Look at Article I, Section 8, and Paragraph 17. It tells us exactly what lands it should have control over. In the same breath it also says that the federal government should not take any land in any state without the consent of the Legislature of that State. Most all these real estate's became government owned through Presidential Proclamations and Executive Orders; now, today, under the guise of the Bureau of Land Management, National Parks Service and the Forest Service the federal government is the largest land baron in the country. Because of that states have been crippled from their ability to prosper from our state's abounding resources.

I would encourage us all to listen to former governors Hammond and Hickel. They have suggested some things I think are worth shuffling with. And how about this Congressman from Georgia? He is starting an intrepid movement to abolish the income tax and the IRS. I think, however, he may suggest a flat tax. The flat tax may work, however abolishing the income tax and IRS is a step in the right direction.

Study American history and the taxing evolution; if we learn anything from this we may begin to focus on correct principles and get back in line with the judicious thoughts and visions of the Founding Fathers.

I have said this once or twice: sometimes we may need to go back if we want to move forward and one of the things we need to go back to is what I have talked considerably about in the onset of this work: Let's go back to abiding by the Natural Laws.

THE COMMERCE CLAUSE

Sunday, December 28, 2003

I have always wondered about that "commerce clause" in the U.S. Constitution. It became clear to me when tribes in Alaska were troubled about Senator Ted Steven's riders in next year's appropriations bill. This measure is designed to regionalize funding to tribes in Alaska. His idea is to seep the funds through regional corporations with the idea the money would trickle into rural communities. Many tribal leaders assume that this is his way of doing away with tribes; with this effort tribal sovereignty and self-governance will be threatened. He also contends that there are too many tribes in Alaska and that he cannot keep them all solvent by funding them on an individual basis.

  The Alaska Federation of Natives (AFN) folks have been dealing with this regionalization issue for some time now; however tribal government leaders don't think AFN has the authority to do this on their behalf and that the Alaska Intertribal Council (AITC) is the organization that should position itself to better advocate on behalf of tribes since it was organized for that purpose. In fact, many tribal leaders were unhappy when a member of the AFN staff came to an AITC Convention and gave an update of their dealings with the Senator on the matter. Last month NCAI discussed this at length and made resolutions supporting Alaska's opposition to Steven's riders. The anxiety here is that if it happens in Alaska it could happen to tribes in the south 48.

The BIA funnels funds to tribes, but this was not an issue during their Providers Conference in early part of December. During the week of December 8th, the AITC had their convention; the AITC it is believed to be the one organization that should represent tribal governments was, indeed, a copious issue as tribal leaders deliberated this problem.

David Case, an attorney and expert on Indian law, gave a presentation on the first day of the convention. He emphasized that tribes in Alaska have always been in existence, and that the land claims did not extinguish tribes. So, we can assume, also, that tribes will always exist.

Mr. Case also articulated the fact that Indian tribes were mentioned only once in the U.S. Constitution. The "commerce clause", indeed, did put tribes in the same category as nations and states. In other words, the federal government must treat tribes as sovereign entities. Of course, many feel this special relationship was never practiced other than the fact that "they sold us liquor, got us drunk and then took our land" as one tribal person stated.

When Ada Deer, former Assistant Secretary of the Department of Interior during President Clinton administration, published in the federal register a list of federally recognized tribes, this strengthened the relationship significantly. Now the feds would have to actually work with tribes on a government to government relationship. This is an important tool tribes can use to erase any notion that the senator, or Congress for that matter, may instigate to regionalize or do away with tribal governments in Alaska.

It was also revealed during the AITC convention that tribes can provide services to their tribal members much better and cheaper than if funds were to trickle from a regional corporation. Another tribal leader said that if President Bush wants to privatize many of its government programs, the way to do it with tribes is to keep things under tribal control.

Tribes have experienced regionalization of funds in the past from the old way the BIA functioned. In the early 1990's the Self Governance Demonstration Project corrected that and since it became permanent in

1994 the BIA has been turning more of its programs, functions, services and activities to tribes.

Yes, I think the "commerce clause" and the recognized tribal government list in the federal register go hand in hand. If Senator Stevens wants to take away that special relationship tribes benefit from the federal government, he is going to have to repeal, by amendment, Article 1, Section 8, paragraph 3 of the U.S. Constitution. A Senator, all by his lonesome, cannot do that. To amend the U.S. Constitution the proposal will have to be passed by both houses, and then ratified by two thirds of the states.

A humongous task indeed.

HISTORY OFFERS LESSON ON HOME SITE PROGRAM

August 25, 1995

The intent of the Founding Fathers of this nation was to guarantee to every citizen under the protection of this country their freedom and liberty. The Declaration of Independence made these principles quite clear. As far as I can see, there is no real room for misinterpretation. It states that the purpose of forming the American republic was to set up a system of government which would guarantee us the protection of our lives, our liberties and our properties, a guarantee which encompasses our right to pursue happiness. It clearly states that when this government grows to such a proportion where it no longer accomplishes these means then it will be time to abolish or alter that government and form a new one based on those same principles. These freedoms are guaranteed to every American under the authority of the Constitution—even us—the first Americans and Alaska Natives.

Life, liberty and ownership of property are an inalienable right. "Inalienable right" means, as I understand it, a natural right. A natural right is a right that cannot be taken away from you because it is something that comes from the Natural Laws or from the Creator himself.

The Constitution guarantees us the right to our life—to live it without fear of another person infringing on that right. It also guarantees us the right to our liberties—that is the right to speak or write whatever we want, the right to worship whomever or whatever our conscience dictates without persecution or interference from the government; the right to do whatever we see fit with our lives so long as we do not interfere with the right of others to do the same thing.

The Constitution also guarantees us the right to the ownership of property and to use that property for our benefit in whatever way we see fit.

It is interesting to note that Article I, Section 8, Paragraph 17 of the Constitution did not authorize the federal government to hold title to land, yet under the guise of the U.S. Forest Service, the National Parks Service, and the Bureau of Land Management, the federal government is the largest land baron in the country.

The federal government, in its earlier days, was given the responsibility to manage the land, but the Constitution did not authorize it to control land through holding title to it.[46] The land really belongs to the American people. Private ownership of property must be secured, or liberty and freedom will not exist.

Article IV, Section 4 of the Constitution states that the United States shall guarantee to every state in this nation a republican form of government[47] and that it can make rules for the government and regulation of land. We like to refer ourselves as a democracy, which is a government in which the majority of the people rules. America is not really a pure democracy—it is a republic, which is defined as a representative limited form of government. We elect representatives to perform services that we cannot do for ourselves. The Founders felt that the less government we have to contend with the better off we will be. Anything than the protection of our lives, liberty and pursuit of happiness is usurpation or oppression.

The Declaration also states that when government fails to perform these duties then the people are obligated to abolish that government and form a new one based on those same principles—that is frame a government that will go back to the principles of protecting our lives,

---

[46] Article I Section 8, Paragraph 14 of the U.S. Constitution
[47] See Do We Live In A Democracy in this work

our liberties, and our pursuit of happiness. Let me emphasize that the Declaration is very clear on that concept and I don't think that there is any other interpretation, whether one believes in the strict or loose interpretation of the Constitution.

In the earlier days of the republic it may have been ambiguous as to how the federal government should have treated our ancestors—the first Americans. To the Anglo-Saxon, we were uneducated savages, therefore they saw fit to formulate and develop policies to deal with the Indians. It was a difficult task to fit us anywhere because of our close relationship to our land, our culture and traditions, our subsistence way of life. These habits were not compatible with the so-called "American way." Many policies were to come forth. We are familiar with many of them: extermination to assimilation or acculturation, to removal or termination, to Indian reorganization to relocation to self-determination and finally self-governance.

Now the Constitution is supposed to guarantee us the right to the ownership of property. The American Indians and Alaska Natives were the first American and, because of that, I believe we have the right to re-claim title to all lands that belonged to us since time immemorial.

We managed to accomplish some of this through the Alaska Native Claims Settlement Act, and as a result were able to, as a group, be awarded the largest land claim settlement ever given to Native Americans. The Constitution guarantees us the same rights as provided for any other American. However, for us as shareholders of village corporations, section 1407 of the Alaska National Interest Lands Conservation Act allows ANCSA corporations to provide each original shareholder up to 1.5 acres of tax free land on which to build a home or to establish a business. As of this date there is no village corporation that has a land distribution program because of legal problems which some people have been identified and use as excuses to not distribute any land. These problems have become so serious that many corporations have been discouraged from developing a shareholder home site program. The sad fact is that because this home site program is under ANILCA and not under ANCSA, the legislative termination date was December 18,

1991. This is the same date on which the ANCSA restrictions were to be removed. When the recent amendments were added to ANSCA, the extensions were not applied to the home site program because it was under ANILCA.

So, when December 18, 1991 arrived and if our village corporations don't have a land distribution policy we will no longer have the option of becoming private land owners. As of this date there is a resolution with the Alaska Federation of Natives to extend section 1407 of ANILCA. Because all of the corporations will not be able to develop a land distribution policy in fourteen months we should support this resolution and write our Alaskan Delegation and let them know how important this matter is to our well-being and survival. Then we will need to show our boards of directors how important this issue is, so they can set this as a number one priority on their "things to do" agenda.

Again, allow me to emphasize a point which has already been expressed above: the land really belongs to the American people. We as Alaskan Natives are as American as American can be. With my understanding of the Constitution I don't believe the federal government has the authority to control our land by holding title; neither does our ANSCA Corporation as it is provided under section 1407, or ANILCA. With that we have the right to insist that our constitutional rights have afforded us.

We need to insist that our board of directors begin working on a policy the day before yesterday so that those shareholders who want land for home sites can be given the opportunity to be a proud Americans and own property of their own.

INTENT IS THE KEY TO FINDING TRUTH

March 10, 2009

Some time ago I came to an important conclusion: one does not have to be a lawyer to understand the U.S. Constitution. If one is honestly exploring for truth about our governmental system we are going to have to look for elements of truth that was intended by the Founding Fathers. Even more so for every document, we need to understand what the intent was for its conception. Purpose should be the underlying factor when one reviews any instrument; one of the things I have tried to do in my study of the Constitution was to keep some of those fundamental principles the Founders had pretty much at the center of my attention.

There are some amendments to the constitution that changed its intent to a great, even dangerous, degree; the Founders warned us about many, the Sixteenth Amendments being one of them. If we keep the Federalist Papers at your elbows you will have learned what Alexander Hamilton, James Madison, and John Jay had to say just about anything regarding the functions of governments. Also, Thomas Jefferson's *Works* is overflowing with much detail on these issues. Jefferson felt that giving the federal system the power to tax was the power to destroy. Thus, were born my articles about the federal governments' ability to impose taxes on our incomes.[48] The premise was that once a central government

---
[48] See The Power To Tax The Power To Destroy, and States Should Have Taxing Powers

was given the authority to tax our paychecks the enactment of such a proposal will invariably lead to the decline of a nation. Collecting from the people's hard-earned labor and placing it in a common, leaky pot to redistribute the wealth never worked in any role during the recorded account of the world. Other stately nations have tried which ultimately prompted people into believing the government owed them a living. Corruption and immorality poisoned those societies to dismal descent. Prime examples are the downfalls of Greece, the Roman Empire and Spain. Today we can use the examples of Canada, Great Britain, Sweden, Greece and, France to identify a few.

The Founders felt strongly that taxing powers should be reserved for states and local governments. In reality look at how and why, today, states and local governments aren't keeping their coffers replenished. The federal system has robbed them of the ability to prosper from their own resources and so we have our hands held out to the federal governments' so-called good intentions. Because our wants are so great, we keep electing people to Congress who will promise us more and more and more———.[49] Also one does not have to become a history don to understand the saga of the world. If we were good learners, we would find out how much of America's chronicles are not told in the classrooms. In particular, there is a huge gap, when America was being born, about the influence the Native Americans had on the framing of the Constitution. The Founders copied the system of the Six Confederate Tribes of the Iroquois nation. Here is an example of what they imitated:

In the Confederacy everything began from the Tribal Councils. The next level was a group called the Younger Brothers, which correlates with our own House of Representative; then there were the Elder Bothers whose functions were the same as our Senate: and then there were the Fire keepers, who served as administrators. When a tribe had reason to wage war with another tribe the War Chief lead his warriors into battle; this is where the concept of the Secretary of Defense comes in.

---

[49] The progressive movement we hear so much about today in America is dangerous—very dangerous.

If thumbs down were given not to go to war then the issue was turned over to the Peace Chief to diplomatically settle the dispute; again we see how the office of Secretary of State was born.

    I am neither an attorney or have a degree in history; I am a simple English major who, because of that discipline, has learned how to learn. I spend a lot of time studying the Constitution, researching history, pondering on these things and appealing to the Creator for guidance. My objective for this process is to find out the reasoning and purpose the Founders envisioned for America and, in many cases, how far we have drifted from their actual intent. Hopefully my articles will stir our minds and inspire people who care into embracing ingenuous values these men demonstrated when this new nation was born—especially when these same values are lacking in our society today and should be restored.

INDIAN SELF-GOVERNANCE

March 1994

April 4th-6th Indian tribes from across the nation assembled in San Diego, California to further evaluate what has been called a tribal Self Governance Demonstration Project. Because of this demonstration, which has been going on since 1991, tribes will decide whether to create a new office in the federal government: The Office of Self Governance (OSG). Tribes will also consider admitting the Indian Health Service into the idea of compacting. Now what will this new office do, and how will it affect tribal affairs with federal functions as we know it today? The main issue in the past was the problems with the bureaucratic function of the BIA

Although some tribal leaders are saying they are not "finger-pointing" at the bureau, others feel the BIA is the "root of the problem" because the bureau pulls the purse strings and "He who pulls the purse strings always has the final say." So, Title III, PL 100-422, the Self-Governance Demonstration Project came into being through a "Tribally-driven" initiative which was made possible through a Congressional authorization. Congress also appropriated funds to support the project.

The reason Self-Governance was proposed as an amendment to P.L. 93-638, which we know as the Indian Self Determination and Education Assistance Act because 638 contracting became such a bureaucratic nightmare that it was near impossible for tribes to receive funds in a timely manner, so they could effectively provide services to communities or tribes. Despite much efforts to try and resolve the problems the BIA was unwilling to change its function as a service provider and manager of tribal affairs to an administrator of government contracts, which was what P.L. 93-638 was all about. It took months after a tribe had submitted their grant applications before they received funding—not only that, but some tribes weren't receiving their full share.

One effort to reform the BIA was "Section 209" which was an addendum to the Indian Self-Determination Act. This was initiated by the Department of Interior and would have provided for a direct transfer of service to tribes with a waiver of Trust Responsibility of the United States. This did not meet well with tribes because of the trust responsibility issue. So, tribes assembled often to offer solutions. Thus, was born Title III, P.L. 100-472 kwon as the Self-Governance Demonstration Project of which seven tribes became the first participants. This concept allowed tribes to set up their own programs yet still hold the federal government accountable for trust responsibilities.

One of the problems with 638 contracting was the sometimes-unfair ways funds were distributed to tribes. Some tribes were receiving more than their contracts provided and others were getting short-changed. I don't know how this was occurring, but this issue was brought forth in many of the discussions during these conferences. One major concern regarding this was that smaller tribes are the ones who suffered while the bureaucratic red-tape was still functioning in the BIA. It was their feeling the bureau was not feeling the effects of this short-change. The mood of the tribes was that to correct the problem tribes will have to find a way in which to eliminate many of the functions of the BIA. Thus, is the reason for creating the Office of Self-Governance.

With the creation of a Self-Governance Office tribes will then be able to negotiate their grants contracts on a genuine government-to-government basis, and instead of receiving a line item grant they will receive a lump sum to run their programs. Additionally, they will be able to receive their funding instantly instead of a matter of months.

So, at the request of tribes Congress provided funding for FY91 to establish an Office of Self-Governance. There were seven tribes who were chosen to participate in the Demonstration Project. The outcome of this was a new policy which was initiated to begin a change in the federal bureaucracy. In June of 1991, after the Office of Self-Governance was established, the elder President Bush made this statement:

"An Office of Self-Governance has been established in the Department of Interior and given the responsibility of working with tribes to craft creative ways of transferring decision-making powers over Tribal government functions from the Department to the Tribes."

The first tier Demonstration Project has proven very useful. In January of 1992 ten more tribes interred into first year Agreements of which Tlingit-Haida Central Council and Kawerak Inc., both of Alaska, were included. This is called a second tier, and in the future there will be more tribes involving themselves in these Compact Agreements. Also, in tier two were five smaller tribes in Southeast Alaska, the Yakutat Tlingit Tribe being one of them. This is how I got involved in the early years of the self-governance programs and what kept me involved for twelve years as President—instead of eight months.

The BIA has been in the process of restructuring their programs to fall more in line with the self-governance concept, and now the Indian Health Service is interested in entering into compact agreements with tribes across the nation. During this conference they came with a proposed list of tribes they wanted to begin working with. For Alaska they suggested it be composed of one package rather than with individual tribes. Southeast East Alaska Regional Health Consortium has been servicing the southeast area and is trying to figure out how they will fit into the scheme of things if the proposal is accepted.

Even though tribes may have differences in many issues the Self-Governance idea has spirited a movement that will set the stage for the reinstatement of what Native Americans have had since time immemorial, a natural right that has been taken away by the federal system, but is now emerging as a new concept that is as old as the picture of civilization itself; the ability to govern themselves.

During the Termination era of federal Indian Policy, Felix S. Cohen wrote an article that appeared in a publication called <u>The American Indian</u> in 1949. In his opening paragraph he says:

"Not all who speak of self-government mean the same thing by the term. Therefore, let me say at the outset that by self-government I mean that form of government in which decisions are made not by the people who are wisest, or ablest, or closest to some throne in Washington or in heaven, but, rather by the people who are most directly affected by the decisions. I think that if we conceive of self-government in these matter-of-fact terms, we may avoid some confusion."

Taking this statement, the question is asked: Is Indian Self-Governance long over-due, or are we interring into it at the right time? Danny Jordan from the California Hoopa Valley Tribe says that it is long over-due, and he emphasizes the fact that all we are doing is "taking back what we have lost but always had since time immemorial."

Indeed, Indian Self-Governance is long over-due. The U.S. Senate and House Bills to make the Self Governance Demonstration Project a permanent are expected to be made law this month. On April 29, 1994 President Clinton has extended an invitation to all tribal leaders to the signing of those bills.

But wait a sec. What are we doing here? Are we creating another monster? Is there another bureaucracy in the making here?

We shall see. Governments, whether they be tribal, local, state or national are only as good as we the people, by the people and for the people, make them. The concept of self-governance or, sovereignty, has been a long debate among our people of late, and it is a noble one if we can keep our perspective in the right direction as we understand more and more about this sleeping giant. It could, in my opinion, set the stage for righting many wrongs not only made against Native Americans, but against all the people in this nation as well.

WE NEED LAWS BASED ON COMMON SENSE

One of the early lessons I learned about the law was that it should be based upon common sense. We are supposed to be living in a republic which I understand to be a limited form of government. Even though we claim that our society is democratic, which means that the majority rules, I now wonder where common sense has gone.

Two routine questions I used to ask myself were: Why is our federal government so huge that its agencies are now entering our daily lives? And now, more recently, I am wondering about our boards and commissions.

For instance, if I fished and hunted to sustain my family and allowed my catches to be unattended to a point where the meat is unusable, the law says that I would be cited for wanton waste. I have no problem with that or with anyone who would commit such an irresponsible act against man and nature. If, however, the law takes exception to the rule and encourages itself to commit the act, then we are dealing with a very serious situation indeed.

A case in point regards the halibut fishery and a regulation the International Pacific Halibut Commission imposed upon people of whom they, in reality, should be serving. This incident happened during the days of the short forty-eight-hour commercial halibut fishery in Alaska. I am a small operator and since 1984 have been involved in the commercial halibut fishery. Several years ago, I set out six skates (longlines) during one of the spring openings. After setting my gear a storm came and drove us smaller boats into port. It was two days before the weather was calm enough to tend to the gear.

About two hours before the closure I encountered a state fish and game officer at the harbor. I informed him about my situation and that I didn't think I'd be able to pull my long lines before the closure. It would take nearly an hour to get to the gear and I would probably only be able to pull two or three skates. "What is the regulation on such a situation?" I asked.

His answer was like this: "You may go out and haul your gear until twelve noon when the season for this period is closed. At this point you may bring your catch in for delivery to the processor. Then you can go back out and retrieve the rest of your gear, but you must release all the halibut whether they are dead or alive."

I was half done with my second skate when twelve noon came. I had about twelve hundred pounds of halibut, all very much alive, which I gutted, cleaned and delivered to the processor.

The next day I pulled the rest of my gear whereupon I released another twelve hundred pounds of near dead halibut, yet in excellent condition. Doing this didn't make sense to me.

A few days later I called the Fish and Game Department and expressed my concern. "Isn't this wanton waste? I asked.

I was told that it wasn't because that was what the International Pacific Halibut Commission had sanctioned. Because of that it is not considered wanton waste? I could not believe what I was hearing! I was taught to believe that we shouldn't let government do what we would be thrown in jail for.

It just didn't make sense! Here a regulation had been made, supposedly, for the purpose of protecting the resource and I had thrown back into the deep over a thousand pound of halibut that I knew would never be able to revive themselves. Yet under other circumstances, if I were caught doing the very same thing, I would be tried and convicted for wanton waste.

Where oh where did common sense go?

During the course of our conversation the question of a regulation made where halibut fishermen would be able to keep what had been caught during the period of the opening season, if for some reason, such as a storm, prevented the retrieving of the gear until after the closure. This made sense to me because the halibut had been caught during the opening period and had remained on the hooks until a time, reasonable of course, when they would be hailed in. I felt this would be a better option, under the circumstance, namely because the halibut had been caught during the opening and, because of an act of God, had been unable to haul the gear during the normal business hours. It only made sense to realize that the fisherman should be held faultless and no one should be allowed to hold him accountable until a reasonable time had transpired.

To throw away thousands of pounds of halibut is truly wanton waste in its purest sense. It does not enhance the program, nor does it protect the resource, which is the purpose of boards and commissions. Isn't it?

It was the opinion of the fish and game official that such latitude would not be in the best interest of the resource because there would be a few fishermen who would abuse the opportunity. But if enforcement was strictly adhered to then, in time, it shouldn't be much of a problem. His thought was a few who would abuse it would make it bad for others.

Again, I wondered where common sense was. A majority of fishermen are honest and want to see justice rendered here, but why must it be at the expense of those who legitimately make their living off this resource? We want to enhance the supply because this is the way we will be making our living for many years to come. We certainly don't want to be responsible for depleting the reserves. It is sad that only a few make it difficult for others and the honest must pay the penalties of the dishonest.

The way I understand it is that government was instituted among men for protecting our lives, our liberties and our properties and to afford us the opportunity to pursue happiness. I also understand that to pursue happiness means that we can enjoy the ownership of property and to use that property in whatever way we wish, so long as we don't interfere with the right of others to do the same. Or it means that we can engage ourselves in any occupation we feel qualified to perform so long as we don't interfere with the right of others to do the same. To put it in a nutshell it means that we can do anything with our lives so long as we don't interfere with the right of others to pursue and achieve happiness. It would have made me very happy if I were to benefit from the Natural Law. The Constitution of the United States guarantees us certain fundamental rights and one of those rights is to be able to provide a decent living for ourselves and our families.

It is true that we elect representatives to do for us what we can't do for ourselves, but do some of these appointive offices, boards and commissions really lose sight of the real purpose of their being?

Is it too late to suggest we go back to the fundamentals? Laws and regulations should make sense. Our laws and regulations ought to be designed to allow every opportunity for the individual to succeed within the bounds of the law.

But again, aren't there too many laws these days? When we get overburdened with laws we find it very difficult to make a move—not knowing whether we are breaking the law or not. Doesn't this violate the idea that we live in a republican form of government? The very simple fact is that government should protect us. We, who are the watch dogs of our legislatures and people who represent us on boards and commissions should not be allowed to do anything that we, as individuals, would be thrown in jail for. I realize that the halibut commission is an international entity, but there are people from the United States who are serving on the commission. They should be champions of that concept. Our government, our boards, our commissions should set the example legislating correct principles.

They should be up there on the pedestal.

They should be there for us to admire and respect and be proud of.

That, I believe is a simple fact that certainly makes sense to me.

But really, where has common sense vanished to these days? What enabled us to knowingly, or unknowingly, violate the law of nature?

WE NEED TO THINK LIKE THE FOUNDERS

December 8, 2009

Jamison Paul's article of June 10th in the Empire articulates his reasons why he thinks our Founding Fathers told us a lie about our unalienable rights to life, liberty and pursuit of happiness. I, for one, am grateful the Founders had the vision to afford each American the opportunity to pursue happiness. They realized that government can't make these things happen; it can only guarantee us these opportunities. They were deliberate enough to realize that not all Americans would be equal politically, socially or economically. They left these pursuits for us to strive for. It's up to us as individuals, as communities and states to bring these noble concepts to fruition; when we do our part our nation becomes that beacon to the world.

In many ways we are our own worst enemies, aren't we? The next sentence in the Declaration of Independence that Mr. Paul states goes on to warn us that mankind is more disposed to suffer under the rules of a malevolent government then to stand up and right themselves by altering or abolishing those forms of government that jeopardizes our freedoms. We are our own worst enemies in this respect because we tend to let things happen to us.

We are no longer cultivated enough to realize that it is up to us to decide when to alter and or abolish. As I said before in this column, I don't believe we are at a point where we need to abolish our government(s) just yet, however we do have a lot of altering to do.

We don't have to stand by and let government dictate to us what we should do. Wars have been fought because people have tried it. We are a nation of laws founded upon the Natural Law, and we should, in no way, let government do what we, ourselves, might be thrown in jail for.

In a republican form of government, the government doesn't tell us what to do. We are delegators in that we dictate to our representatives how we want government to function so that we can enjoy our freedoms—nothing more or nothing less. We tell government what to do so that we can enjoy the fruits of our labor without too many rules or regulations.

A republic is a representative type of government with limited powers. We are supposed to elect good people to represent us in the affairs of government and they use the democratic format to conduct business for our best interest.

We will always be confronted with challenges like prejudice, civil disobedience, skin heads, socialistic ideas, special interest groups, environmentalists, progressivism—you name it; you can even start your own. But when anything threatens our freedom we should not sit on the fence and see what side the coin will fall. Freedom, and standing up for our liberties, means taking a proactive approach to our problems.

We shouldn't let things happen to us. We are a free nation of people and to maintain our freedom we need to be diligent in our pursuit of happiness.

How do we recognize these threats and what can we do?

I think we need to think like the Founding Fathers. They were the ones who set the stage for the protection of our lives, our liberties and our pursuit of happiness. These fundamental principles were formulated from the Natural Law because they understood the Natural Law. In the earlier days of our republic the little red school houses taught the children the principles embedded in the U.S. Constitution. They took it apart piece by piece, interpreted it, and put it back together again. The reason was so that if ever it came time to they would be able to defend our republic when it was threatened, not by the sword but by words based upon correct principles.

How many of our children can recite the Preamble of the Constitution these days?

Self-determination, like freedom, needs to be relentlessly fought for, whether it is on the battlefield in a foreign country or on the home front. This struggle has been going on since the time of man's first manifestation and will continue until the only remaining man, or women, stands on the front line and valiantly goes down defending our families in the name of liberty.

And so, if we could look at the Constitution in constructive ways perchance we may begin to utilize those principles the Founders documented for us.

But we need to start thinking like them; then perhaps, we can begin to make important alterations to our governmental systems that may become detrimental to our freedoms.

WHERE DOES GOODNESS COME FROM?

September 1, 2002

I was going to stay away from this topic, but I think, now, that I must express my opinion on the matter. It is this question of God being taken from the Pledge of Allegiance. I understand that many of the Founding Fathers of this country did not believe in a supreme being. However, it is a pretty well-known that when they locked themselves in Constitution Hall to plan the formation of this new nation they, indeed, opened and closed their meetings appealing for guidance from the Almighty. I have to say I sincerely believe these men were raised up by Providence for the purpose of birthing a nation that was destined to serve as an ensign to the world. At the time America needed this - and America surely needs it now.

There is this beautiful painting of George Washington kneeling in prayer in the middle of the winter at Valley Forge. The story behind this painting was never elaborated much about in the textbooks. We know his men were starving and ill clothed; we also know many were killed and just as many had deserted. In fact, Washington had become disheartened himself. However, during this dismal spell he was prompted to appeal to the Creator. There was this vision General Washington had during this special moment. The image was that of a dark cloud which hovered over America. Then the cloud evaporated and brightness radiated the homeland. With this revelation the Father of this nation was able to gather his troops and not only win battles but eventually win the war. This incident changed the course of history for all mankind. Think of it for a moment. If he hadn't seen this vision what do you suppose he might have decided during one of America's darkest moments?

God is mentioned in the Declaration of Independence five times. In the first paragraph of the Declaration it plainly states that the American people should pay attention to the Law of Nature and Nature's God. I think the most significant is where it says that we are all endowed by the Creator with certain unalienable rights. This means that our rights are derived from Nature and God, and that among these are the right to the protection of our lives, our liberties, and our pursuit of happiness.

It really says that.

Read it.

It's very clear.

In the second to the last paragraph there is mention that the Founders appealed to the Supreme Judge of the world and in the last paragraph they admitted that they relied on the protection of Divine Providence to guide them through troubled times.

Alexis de Tocqueville was a French political scientist who was commissioned by his government to visit America in the mid-1800s. His regime wanted to know why this country rose to such prominence in such a short period of time in comparison to other great nations that have come and gone. He found his answers when he visited the homes, the schools and churches. In the homes he saw family solidarity where people worked together. In the schools he witnessed students studying the Constitution. Teachers were having them take it apart and put in back together again. They needed to understand it so that if they had to they would be able to defend the republic. In the churches he saw the spiritual strength of America. In 18 months, he completed his visit and returned to France to write this book called "Democracy in America."

You ought to read it. In it he wrote, "America is great because America is good." What a statement! Where does this goodness come from? I think it comes from God.

And then he also said, "America will cease to be great only when it ceases to be good." The spiritual strength of America was derived from God-given principles.

So fine - take God out of the Pledge of Allegiance. However, we cannot deny that He is assuredly in the credentials that set the standard for the world to draw from as a model for decency and goodness. Are we going to allow that to be taken away too?

Well, we may allow God to be taken from our institutions, but to true Americans, never from our hearts, never from our roots, and never from the nurture of our spiritual well-being.

AMERICA STANDS FOR GOODNESS

At a very young age during the middle part of World War II I began to understand a little bit about wars and rumors of wars and it was then that I began to sense that America was a very special home to me. It was like when I found out what an American Indian was and that I was one. I was plumped with pride. And then when the Second World War was over—I really thought Americans were special even more so because we had triumphed over great odds.

As I have studied history over a number of decades there are several documents and books that have helped me understand what we, as Americans, are all about. Foremost, of course, are the Declaration of Independence and the Constitution of the United States. I have made this evident in previous articles and will continue to do so to the end of my days.

Marcus Tillis Cicero helped me gain an important idea of what the Natural Law is. I know, now, that the Natural Law is the Creator's order of things— that it is unchangeable and applies to every nation, kindred, tongue and people. When we go against the Law of Nature bad things happen.

The Federalist Papers have been a great help with understanding what the Founding Father's real intent of the Constitution was designed for.

And then there was this treatise called *The Law* by Frederic Bastiat (1801-1850) a French economist and statesman. He did most of his writing before and after the French Revolution of 1848; early in is adult career he began to see the dangers of socialism and how it was creeping into the French political structure. In his book he constantly refers to the socialistic doctrine and how it would eventually translate into communism. The book also appealed to me because it tells how great nations have come and gone and shows how we can see the dangers of a decline by studying the rise and fall of civilizations. I believe many American statesmen should be interested in this dissertation as well. One important fact that Mr. Bastiat emphasized was that our rights come from God. When I thought about this I concluded that no government, or government entity, has the power to take that unalienable right from us.

Now another book that had a great impact on me was Democracy in America by Alexis de Tocqueville (1805-1859); I have quoted passages from his book on occasion. He came to America at the direction of the French government in the mid 1800's to learn how America became such a great nation. When he finished his nearly two-year investigation, he went back to France and wrote this three-volume book. He found out how America became what it is when he visited families and went into the schools and churches of America.

In the schools he discovered that students were taking the fundamentals of the constitution apart and putting it back together to better understand how the Founders had designed it. The purpose for doing this was to know what America stood for. If, and whenever, they had to defend the republic they would be able to do so without going to war or disintegrating our social order.

Tocqueville also discovered the spiritual strength in America when he visited the churches across the country. Here he saw how the structure of communities was based on the spiritual might of individual families. He believed that America was great because America was good, and that America would cease to be great only when it ceased to be good. He also came to the realization that religion did not play a direct role in the governments in America, yet he emphasized that religion had to be the most important institution in the lives of the people, the spiritual strength of the governmental servants translated to how political people should serve the country's citizens.

My favorite book, I discovered only within the last decade, is called Wampum Belts and Peace Trees. This tells about how the Native Americans influenced the formation of our constitutional government. This book helped me become a proud Native American; and a patriotic one at that.

So where does our freedom come from? The declaration is very clear when it says that it is self-evident that we are endowed by the <u>Creator</u> with certain unalienable rights. God is mentioned in the declaration four more times. This is no fable!

Read it.

It says that! I really don't think there's very much room for interpretation any other way.

Bastiat also emphasized that God is the creator of life and that the gift of life involves our intellect, physical and moral being. He also said that we must take life and constantly try our best to improve it by preserving it, developing it and perfecting it. He ardently believed that God gave us this earth to assist us in these efforts.

The American republic was raised for the purpose of being an ensign for liberty to the world. When people see the American flag, it is representative of the symbol for freedom and liberty. So, when people desecrate or burn it—what are they doing?

I have said before—I am convinced Providence, indeed, did rise up good men to organize this country for the sake of decency. No other nation has risen to such heights as the United States has. And we did it in less than 50 years! It took other great democracies that have come and gone hundreds of years to reach their pinnacle of successes! Imagine that if you will.

Freedom has been threatened by the likes of the Stalin's, the Hitler's, the Mussolini's, and modern-day tyrants like Osama Bin Laden, and Saddam Hussein and today ISIS. We are not just fighting tyrants—we are combating evil. America, indeed, in its true form does stand for goodness.

Yes—we are a great nation—and to go to war or not to go to war is an issue that is foremost in the thoughts and hearts of the American people. With these challenges ahead of us in the next few days and weeks months, even years—we can be even greater. However, our greatness will always be measured in proportion to our goodness.

COMBATING DEPENDENCY, A CHALLENGE FOR NATIVE COMMUNITIES

October 25, 1994

Call to Action: Taking Community Responsibility was the theme of the Alaska Federation of Natives (AFN) pre-conference workshop held on October 10th and 11th. The mission was to identify items Native Councils in Alaska, families and individuals can do to improve life for people without asking permission or funding from government to do so.

Inspired by the Alaska Native Commission's Final Report[50], village tribal leaders were challenged to identify grass roots reliance not only with chemical dependency, but with Native dependency upon the government dole.

Like a substance abuser, breaking dependency on welfare programs will not be an easy task. Analogous to one who is dependent upon alcohol, or one who is hooked on drugs, one must realize, and admit, that he or she has a problem with addiction. Usually this is discovered when one hits the bottom of the pit; not wanting to perish in the gutter the only way out is for someone to haul you up.

Participants of the conference ardently discussed how alcohol/drugs (even tobacco) is perilous to health and suggested the AFN Convention propagate resolutions directing tribal or village councils to ban alcohol

---

[50] See Testimony before the Alaska Native Commission,

and drugs, as well as pass ordinances making bootleggers, moon shiners and drug dealers accessories to crimes committed because of drunkenness or drug dependency. Warranted, for nearly two centuries Native Americans have had this acute problem. Only in recent years have programs been developed to help abusers.

But look at what one has to go through to overcome. First is recognizing a problem, then overcoming denial, getting the necessary help, and then enduring withdrawals. Many have failed going "cold turkey." Even AA programs have not solved the whole problem (admittedly, they have done a tremendous job, however). I understand places like Schick Shadel have a high rate of success; on the other hand, I know some people who have gone through their alcohol program only and are still hooked on drugs.

It's encouraging that Alaska Native Medical Clinic (AMNC) and AFN acknowledged a profound obstacle Natives have been enduring for decades. Dependency on governments to provide a living for us is one of the main reasons why nations of the past have come and gone are gone. Consider the great nations that have risen to great heights since the recorded history of man—none have fallen because of conquest from without; their downfall was because of erosion from within. People become strong because of their love for liberty, the protection of their lives, and their ability to seek happiness without interference from government. A young nation guarantees these to its subjects, and as people prosper they have a tendency to unfold to slipshodness and the nation evolves to dependency on government to solve their problems—even to providing a large majority of its inhabitants with a living. This is really against human nature and the Natural Laws.

Taking from the "haves" and giving to the "have-nots" is not new to civilization. The re-distribution of wealth has never been successful because history has undeniably proven that when a nation goes against the laws of nature bad things happen. When we force, through taxation, the wealthy to contribute to a common pot and that pot is re-distributed to people who are idle those people's incentives are thwarted. As a result, initiatives are stifled and character is embezzled. It is exceptionally difficult to get out of that pit, much less admit that there is a decisive problem, so the hand of the recipient is always out petitioning for more. Politicians eager for your vote will promise you more. You would think civilization would learn from history. These tactics have been tried and they have never worked.

It was agreed among tribal leaders that the first responsibility for solving these dilemmas fall within the individual where it would translate to family and filter into communities. John Schaeffer, long time Native leader, conceded there is a serious problem, but offered that there is still no answer on how we can overcome our dependence. Another prominent Native leader, Perry Eaton, gave a luncheon talk on October 11th—his message about breaking government dependency was very strong. "We have to begin now!" he concluded.

Again, it is heartening to know that Native leaders have recognized the actual problems, and the urge is more than treating the symptom but treating root causes. For some time now, Native leaders have recognized the problem. They realize, also, that many communities will go through a period of denial when these issues are brought out. We will have to face those realities. Once admitted, like a substance abuser, we will be able to start addressing the root causes. Then, if communities are serious about overcoming dependency, we will have to go through "withdrawals." It will take many years for villages to "clean" themselves from these ills.

Once the people are committed to solving the problems, then they will have to work with state and federal governments to educate appropriate agencies on our desires. It is important to find those candidates who have an idea what government really should do for us.

On October 13th, gubernatorial candidates debated at the AFN Convention for the Native vote. The one person who understands what government should really do for us—one, who fittingly answered the questions on Native sovereignty, subsistence, and government responsibilities, will never get elected governor, even though he got a lot of applause for his comments. The contest will be between the democratic and republican candidates, liberals who believe the government has the answers to all our problems and the conservatives who advocate less government.[51] During the debate Green Party candidate, Jim Sykes, answered all the questions candidly. If people really listened, they would have realized he was most politically correct. Furthermore, we didn't listen to the other parties at all. Native minds were already made up as to who they will endorse. We will have to insist our next governor respond to our concerns about getting off the dole and becoming self-sufficient.

The big challenge is for Native leaders to go back to their communities and start the movement. Once communities realize and recognize our problems, then we can begin working on programs to make essential improvements. Once we recognize our dependency (overcoming denial), and once we begin the process of getting off the dole, we will, like the substance abuser, experience "withdrawals." More than any challenge we have experienced in our lives as individuals we will collectively have to stick with the program. We can triumph with this endeavor. I wish all Native communities well and good luck as we set the example for this nation as well.[52]

---

[51] The progressive movement has filtered into both major parties and as a result is not constitutionally aligned anymore—they are concerned about party problems rather than getting

[52] As of this date nothing has been done to work on programs to break away from the federal dole. Instead Alaskan villages, in particular, are reaching out for more hand-outs.

EACH TRIBE MUST CARRY SELF-GOVERNANCE FORWARD

January 1994

Frustration among Indian Tribes across America was expressed at an Indian Health Service Self-Governance Conference in Scottsdale, Arizona.

"We need to walk away from this meeting feeling we have done something," said Henry Cagey, a Lummi tribal leader, and one of the moderators of the meeting. "If we don't get our act together, we'll be doing the same thing thirty years from now."

Two years ago, I attended a Bureau of Indian Affairs (BIA) self-governance conference in Washington, DC, where I was introduced to the self-governance concept. My soul stirred when I learned that it was a tribally driven initiative and contained the basic, fundamental principle that all mankind from the beginning of recorded history to now have been striving to achieve: absolute sovereignty.

Self-governance is the right of tribal governments to determine, for themselves, what programs they want to administer on behalf of their tribal members.

This differs from self-determination contracting in that it does away with the line-item practices that have been exercised in the past. It also does away with the nightmare of negotiated annual funding agreements. Such agreements crawl up the bureaucratic ladder at a snail's pace and back down again before funding is disbursed.

Under self-governance, funding disbursements would be done in a timely manner, enabling tribal governments to make payroll and bill paying obligations without deficit spending.

W. Ron Allen, Chairman of Jamestown S'Klallam Tribe, identified another reason for self-governance. He said, "Self- Governance for us is to foster self-sufficiency. This is a cause worth fighting for."

So where is the frustration in this noble cause? The BIA began a demonstration project in 1990 with seven tribes from various parts of Indian Country participating. Each year about seven tribes entered into the demonstration project. Middle management people from IHS headquarters attended the conference. They came with a hip pocket full of instructions and policies with strict instructions from the department heads.

Joe De La Cruz,[53] a tribal leader from the Quinault Nation, interrupted a heated discussion on why the IHS is confused about self-governance.

"The self-governance idea was a tribally driven," he said. "The concept came from tribes and tribes were successful in pushing it through Congress from a demonstration project to permanent legislation. You restructure your regulations and policies to comply," he said.

Like the BIA during the onset of self-governance, the IHS is experiencing downsizing and adjustment problems. Like the BIA, IHS is having problems with the role of the Office of Self- Governance (OSG).

The BIA had no clout with the Department of Interior. In previous tribal working groups, a proposal was submitted to Bruce Babbitt, Secretary of the Department of Interior, suggesting that the OSG be elevated from Assistant Secretary Ada Deer's office and put under Babbitt's administrative center.

Tribal leaders understood the OSG as an advocate for tribes, but if it doesn't have clout, the office is useless.

W. Ron Allen observed, "We need to envision what OSG's intent was in the beginning. We need to put it where it will make a difference,

---

[53] Mr. De La Cruz died several years ago from a heart attack while waiting at the Seattle airport to fly to a meeting.

and it should be adequately staffed with qualified people." Since it is the opinion of many tribal leaders that Dr. Trujillo is not well versed in the self-governance concept, it follows that it should be placed under Donna E. Shalala, secretary of Health and Human Services; even though she, too, may be lacking in the self-governance concept, tribal leaders feel that direct contact to her would be better than trying to go through an in-between department or person.

Other frustrations tribal people are expressing are many, Cindy Holmes, self-governance coordinator of the James S'Klallam tribe, made a significant observation. "The concept of self-governance was lost through the negotiation process," she said.[54] She feels there is no difference between the so-called 638 self-determination contracting and self-governance compacting these days. "We've evolved back to the 638-negotiation process," she observed.

I am not the only one concerned about where the self-governance process is going. When I first got involved, I cheered those leaders who initiated the demonstration project. National tribal leaders such as Joe De La Cruz, W. Ron Allen, G.I. James and Danny Jordan, were, indeed inspired people. It was they, along with other tribal leaders from sea to shining sea, who gave birth to this tribally driven initiative. They, with the consultation of tribal leaders saw this thing through from beginning to now. However, it is up to individual tribes across the country to carry this idea of self-sufficiency and self-government forward.

When we do, when we catch a glimpse of this quest for people to be sovereign and how to achieve it—and keep it. I envision our people setting the pace for the rest of the non-native country. All the mechanisms are there. We need to embrace that vision from local perspective, and then make it work for us.

Where do we start? Study the final report of the Alaska Native Commission. It tells all and offers solutions.[55]

---

[54] Meaning when tribes negotiate their annual funding agreements with OSG.

[55] See Testimony before Alaska Native Commission and Breaking Dependency—A Challenge for Alaska Native Communities in this work.

PART THREE

THE ALASKA NATIVE BROTHERHOOD

"There is a good chance that all Native organizations may fall, and even if that happens the Alaska Native Brotherhood will be in the forefront fighting for our Native rights."

Cyrus Peck
Past Grand Camp Secretary

ONE OF THE FIRST

It was 1944. I was seven years old and living in Juneau. In those days there were three core educational systems for the youth of Alaska: The Territorial schools for the non-natives, the Bureau of Indian Affairs (BIA) schools for the Natives, and then the private, Christian schools. The schools were segregated, but the Natives wanted their children to have the best education possible, and they were supposed to be regarded as citizens, so Natives believed the schools should be integrated. This crusade had been going on for many years by the Alaska Native Brotherhood and Sisterhood. The two individuals I remember who were in the middle of this cause were Roy Peratrovich and his wife, Elizabeth. However, there was one other individual who made a difference—to me anyway.

My father took a job with a construction company and moved us from Yakutat to Juneau that year. I don't remember much about the political battles which took place in those days, being only seven years old. However, as I matured and learned more about the prejudice that was practiced in Juneau, I was appalled. I was there in the days when there were signs on the public places that read: NO DOGS OR NATIVES ALLOWED. Luckily, I don't remember seeing them because my parents kept us from those places. Yet there was one incident my parents couldn't shield me from.

We lived on 9th street in a brown house my father rented near the Juneau-Douglas Bridge. Moving from Yakutat to Juneau was a new experience for me and my four-year-old brother, but we got acquainted with the neighborhood in a hurry. There were both native and non-natives living in that area. Frank See and his wife, Bessie, and their children lived a couple of houses from us. Across the street and up a way lived Shirley Allstead and her family. She was a beautiful half Native girl and my first crush. I remember my parents being proud when she won the crown as Fourth of July Queen that year.

That summer was a great one for me. I remember playing with my friends, getting into mischief and being grounded and having spankings for more serious offenses. The summer went by quickly and we were involved in many activities. I remember going to baseball games in the park where the federal building now stands, to a soap box derby on the fourth of July, and to the movie Bambi when it was first released. Those were fun days—it seemed that when one looks back on his earlier years one always remembers the good times—never the bad. I always seem to remember the sunny days—those sunny days when we enjoyed picnics and outings that were never really designed to be remembered forever—never the sad, rainy days when we had to stay inside and be bored. I'm sure there were many of those days; but you know, I can't remember days like that.

There is one bad day that I remember though. I have always remembered it, but in my later years when I related it to my friends, they responded like I was telling a tall tale. But I remember well when Roy, who was the Grand Camp President of the Alaska Native Brotherhood, and Elizabeth, who was the Grand Camp President for the Sisterhood, came to see my parents.

Roy and my father got along well. They both had a great sense of humor and were able to tell jokes and stories to one another and not feel threatened.

When Roy and Elizabeth arrived that evening, Roy got right down to business. "John," he said, "As you know the A.N.B. and A.N.S. Grand Camp has been trying to get the B.I.A. and Territorial schools integrated. It has been a tough battle, John, but I think we can win. What we are trying to do is get some parents to register their children in the public schools this year. We are asking if you would be willing," he paused and nodded toward me, "to do this with your child?" Without hesitation my parents accepted the challenge.

And so instead of my mother taking me to the "Indian" school near where the Alaska Native Brotherhood hall is now, she walked me up 9th Street, up a steep hill, past the Governor's Mansion, and to what seemed like a huge structure behind the Territorial building.

I was going into the second grade that year. It was strange because I didn't see any of my friends on the first day of school. I thought of Frank See who had a daughter my age. Her name was Spunky and we became very good friends. In fact, she was probably my first girlfriend, and if I'd stayed around for high school we probably would have gone steady. Anyway, I looked for her and my other friends from 9th Street but couldn't find them anywhere. I found out later that I was one of the three Indian students who showed up for school that day.

My teacher was nice to me and did what she could to help me feel comfortable. Still I kept pretty much to myself.

That was until recess.

We went outside to play, and the teacher was trying to get me to play tag with the other kids. I didn't feel like playing tag, so I sat by myself.

The teacher tried to get me to swing on the swings and bounce up and down on the see-saw, but I didn't want to do either of these things.

I just wanted to sit by myself.

"Hi," a high-pitched voice said. I looked up. There was this girl with red hair in pig-tails. She had these freckles and eyes that were as blue as the sky. She looked down at me and smiled. She had no front teeth, but the smile was friendly. "My name is Amy. Wanna play some jumping jacks?" she asked.

Instantly the ice melted. We played jumping jacks until the bell rang.

We were regular partners in jumping jacks after that.

The next day we played on the swings and see-sawed and played tag. It wasn't long before the other kids were in there playing with us.

One morning we were sitting under a tree playing jumping jacks and this girl came to us. "Do you play with Indians?" she said to Amy.

Amy leaped to her feet and started jumping up and down. "He's not an Indian!" she screamed so that the whole neighborhood could hear. "He's not an Indian!" she repeated. "He's my friend!"

When I went home that afternoon I asked my mother what an Indian was. It was then that I began to get a little education about life—and human relationships.

Today I think about those first days in the territorial school system and wonder what Amy is doing these days.

I can say, however, and with much pride, that I was one of the first to be accepted into the public schools when much prejudice was felt in every part of Alaska.

But Amy, you were the first to accept someone who you recognized wasn't any different from you by a long shot. Your attitude made a huge difference and set the tone for what was to later come. I thank you, along with a host of other people like you, who made it much easier for people like me during that period of very difficult adjustment.

ANB CHAMPIONS FOR NATIVE RIGHTS

1993

In his presentation at an Alaska Native Brotherhood Convention several years ago, Ramsey Clark, former U.S. Attorney General, said something to the effect that there is no organization in existence which would be able to "solve all of the problems of future generations." I craved a chance to set him straight and acquaint him with the Alaska Native Brotherhood, but he vanished before I had a chance to intercept him.

A year or so later I attended an ANB Convention which was held in Sitka that year. Cyrus Peck, one of the Executive Committee members, revealed something that turned out to be significant to me. "When 1991 approaches, there is a chance that all of the corporations might go out of business in a short while," he said. He emphasized that if Sealaska Corporation folded, the Tlingit-Haida organization might, likewise, go down the drain. These collapses would cause a chain reaction which would eventually dissolve our local for-profit native corporations. These collapses would mean we would lose our stock, our land and everything which had identified us as Alaska Natives. He concluded his remarks by maximizing that the ANB will still be with us, that it will be in the forefront fighting for our Native rights and issues.

I believe this to be literally true because the Alaska Native Brotherhood based its foundation upon the love of God and country, the sanctity of the family unit and the strength and loyalty of its members.

When the missionaries came into our villages and began to instruct our people about the principles of Christianity, our people experienced many conflicts—a culture clashes which interfered with our lifestyle and traditions. This "outside" influence, as noble as it might have been, threatened our very existence by taking away our history, culture, traditions and everything that made us Tlingits. The federal government added to this erosion of our well-being by requiring us to become educated. Once again, as noble as this might have been, required that we give up our traditional ways of providing for our families and our villages, thereby transferring us from a **land-based** affluence to a cash economy. When we survived off a land-based economy, we took only what we needed from the rich resources from our territories, while the commercializing of our resources required us to fish and hunt for more than we needed for profit. Competition and greed became the motivating factor in our lives and the transition was distressing and very demanding.

But the missionary messages were potent ones and our people responded to them because, inwardly, they were craving for this kind of knowledge. There was candor contained in the messages of these interlopers which appealed to the sentiment of the Indian folks. There is evidence the American Indians accepted many of the white explorers with open arms when they first appeared in this continent. They believed the leaders of these intruders were the great Prophet who, at one time, came to visit our people many hundreds of years ago. He had promised that he would return, and our ancestors deemed these white men were this white God. Some legends and stories of Indian tribes throughout North and South America detail this visit also.[56]

The story of Raven (Yeil) can be noticed here. Our stories tell that he was sent by a being higher than he on a mission, and when he completed his task of creating a place for the Tlingits to dwell and placed the animals, fishes and birds on the land, and had provided them with the methods and means of taking care of the resources, he was deified and went away to live in a cave near Katella (some people

---

[56] He walked The Americas, L. Taylor Hanson, Legend Press

believe he went to the Nass River). In any event, he promised that he would one day return.[57]

When a Russian schooner first appeared off Lituya Bay, the Tlingits thought it as a white bird (Raven at one time was white) flying over the ocean. It gracefully sailed into Lituya Bay and then as, the white vessel lowered it sails, they believed that it was Raven folding his wings and that he had returned to them as he had promised. They gathered on the shoreline to welcome him back but became disappointed when they saw men approaching them in boats.

There is this book called **He Walked the Americas** that is worth reading for every Native American to see if these legends bring back stories that confirm this visit. So, the acceptance of such a story was not strange to our ethnic group.

There is this man from Angoon—he is over a hundred years old—who tells about the visit of Jesus Christ to his people. There is also a Tshimsian legend which relates the birth of a boy which takes place across the "land of many waters"—winged beings had come to this group of Tshimsian hunters and had manifested this event. These messengers told them that this infant would grow up to redeem the world and that his message would teach the Tshimsians the correct way in which to live and change the lives of many people. A sense of genuineness was felt in the teachings of the missionaries, and for that reason I sincerely believe that this is one of the reasons why the ANB is based upon the principles of Christianity. Our meetings have always opened and closed with prayers to the Creator.

Along with Christianity there is the love of family and country. A belief in the sanctity unit has kept this organization together. The adage that "a family which prays together is a family that stays together" was a philosophy which the ANB and ANS strongly believed. It taught this to its membership in the earlier days, a trait which extended right out of our culture. In the organization there was the school committee, a committee that kept in track of the school systems so that they were assured that the children were attending school and getting the education

---

[57] See Introduction

they needed. There was also the home committee, a committee that kept track of the families and whenever there was a need, sickness, or emergency, the committee was there to lend quick assistance.

Then there is the love of country. Our Founding Fathers were patriotic people who pledged allegiance to the flag and sang America the Beautiful and the Star-Spangled Banner with pride in the same breath as the battle song, Onward Christian Soldiers. Many of our young men, through the years, have proudly served in the armed services and fought in the Second World War. I heard the story told many times about how the builders of the ANB Hall at Yakutat flew "Old Glory" at the bow of the gas boat while it towed the logs from across the bay to the building site. Camp # 13, the Yakutat Camp, was chartered on February 22, 1923. People celebrated Founder's Day along with George Washington's birthday on this day with pride.

The success of the ANB is dependent upon the strength and dedication of its individual members. The power and influence come from the members, and the officers were never thought of as the so-called "masters" of the organization. Instead the officers were regarded as servants and through the democratic process the membership was allowed to express their feelings and desires by discussion and the voting process during meetings. Officers understood that it was their duty to carry out the wishes of the membership. Without brotherhood participation, there is no power or authority. The ANB Constitution never intended the powers of its administrators to be misused, and that is why the association had been so successful in the earlier days. The Founding Fathers had their heads screwed on right.

It is now time for us, as members of this royal formation, to get our heads screwed on right and begin to bring back those principles which made the ANB a powerful and viable institution. This institution was never intended to be feared by our non-native friends—only respected for its fortitude, wisdom, and perseverance.

The Alaska Native Brotherhood, since its beginning, had been a living and influential organization championing Native Rights, and as a result, all peoples of Alaska have benefited because of the tremendous work the organization dedicated to righting wrongs committed against humanity.

Right from its beginning, the ANB has been solving problems for our people and, as Cyrus Peck so eloquently stated at that ANB/ANS Convention many years ago, will continue to do so when all others have failed.

ALASKA NATIVE BROTHERHOOD AND THE INDIAN REORGANIZATION ACT

On the back of their membership cards the Alaska Native Brotherhood claims responsibility, along with a host of other achievements, for bringing the Indian Reorganization Act (I.R.A.) into Southeast Alaska. Yet if one were to look into the history of the I.R.A. concept, he would learn some very important facts that would startle the I.R.A. supporters today. For over ten years the Alaska Native Brotherhood studied, pondered and debated the concept in their annual conventions during the mid-1930 and 40's; but in the end the organization decided against adopting the Wheeler-Howard legislation. There were many reasons for the controversy, but the reality for not accepting the I.R.A. in Southeast Alaska was because, in those days, our leaders thought we would have to accept reservation status[58]. Because of that many thoughts we would be deprived of our citizenship rights, not to mention the fact that strong feelings for and against the idea threatened the credibility of the Alaska Native Brotherhood.

Many of our future leaders had gone to schools out of state such as Chemowa and Charlise boarding schools for Indians, and they were able to see firsthand the segregation and discrimination on the

---

[58] The Native Brotherhoods: Modern intertribal Organizations On The Northwest Coast, P.51+++++++++++++

reservations. They therefore regarded accepting reservation status as a step backward[59]. Witnessing the adverse conditions of their southern counterparts, our former leaders of the A.N.B. could see that they had an opportunity to determine the destiny of future generations and concluded that reservations would not be for our people, neither in those days— nor in the days to come. They felt strongly that becoming a reservation would be "turning back the clock" when, in fact, they had been going away to school to learn how they could improve their condition and status among the human races of the world. Another reason why our former leaders turned "thumbs down" on reservations was they knew that if they were to compete in the white man's world they would have to achieve citizenship status. To qualify themselves for this they knew they had to obtain their education and learn how to use the Anglo-Saxon ideas to improve them. Many of our people got their education and were proud of the fact that they were learning well how to prepare themselves for the future.

Unfortunately, many of our young natives did not find reason to return back to their homes in Alaska, and so relocated in the south forty-eight. As a result, and sadly at that, a lot of these people did not bring their education and expertise back home. However, for those who did, they started a long, hard battle that took many years of their lives, their fortunes and their sacred honors to obtain recognition as U.S. citizens. The right to vote followed, and then we won the equally protracted tug-of-war to get our own people represented in the territorial legislature. All these, and more, were thanks to the Alaska Native Brotherhood.

It was in 1934 when the Wheeler-Howard Act became a heated issue during the A.N.B. conventions. Originally it had been an act brought forth by Congress for Indians in the south forty-eight who resided on reservations[60]. Many people felt it was not applicable to Alaska; however, if Alaskan Natives wanted to take advantage of the act they would have to request that reservations be established. The

---

[59] Abid
[60] Abide, p.52

introduction of the act was made possible in Southeast Alaska through passage of Public Law 538 by the 74th Congress. This caused a great deal of controversy among our people; misunderstanding and suspicion of the Indian Reorganization Act concept persisted, particularly amidst the younger faction. The main issue of the measure was forming reservations; according to the provisions it was a must to receive the benefits of the I.R.A. Many of our people thought that reverting to a reservation was degrading; in no way did they want to be segregated; they prided in their citizenship status and wanted to become a viable part of the civil government of Alaska. The creation of a reservation, they thought, would have resulted in loss of citizenship, an issue that had been a long-drawn-out fight and "tough sledding" to achieve in the first place. Even though the setting aside of tracts of land could have been a positive provision under a reservation status, most of our people did not want to lose their standing as citizens. The assault to win it was too great to relinquish. At this point in time our people were vainly, yet progressively, struggling to establish themselves as equals with the whites and were proud of that reality.

There were, however, another group of people who took the other side of the issue. They were a fair number of the elderly who felt life on the reservation would provide them with more security in the way of government supported medical and welfare care; they also regarded the establishment of the reservation as a sure, and probably, safest way of keeping control of their lands. Now aren't these pretty much the same issues presently being brought to the surface today? (Only these are the younger group of people). In any event, at the beginning, these were a cluster of people who had no desire, or incentive, to compete in the world of the white man.

For many years the question of the reservations and Indian Reorganization Act were heated and bitter discussions during annual conventions. It finally got to a point where the reservation issue was threatening to drastically split the Alaska Native Brotherhood. Over a period they eventually came to the realization that compatibility and solidarity in the Brotherhood should override their differences. So, they decided to "chuck" the reservation idea rather than cause a schism. At the convention of 1946 a resolution was adopted which provided an option for each of the camps in the various communities to make a choice; any community who wanted to take advantage of the I.R.A. can request a reservation be chartered. The Alaska Native Brotherhood was committed to assist in every way to achieve that village's request. If a village did not want a reservation then the A.N.B. would, likewise, see that the reservation idea would not be forced upon it.

In 1936 Congress made an amendment to the act allowing Alaskan villages to participate in the IRA program without becoming a reservation. All they needed to do was officially form a tribal council and a constitution.

So, if the Alaska Native Brotherhood wants to claim they were responsible for bringing I.R.A.'s into Southeast Alaska, then we can conclude that it was equally responsible for opposing it as well. The over-riding factor, however, was that the Alaska Native Brotherhood did not officially endorse, nor encourage, the Indian Reorganization Act; it only offered assistance to any village that wanted it, and discouraged attempts to have it forced upon any community that did not want it.

It was not until these past few years that the I.R.A. concept, once again, emerged as a controversial issue in our conventions; and for the very same reasons our former leaders discussed, pondered and debated to death in their conventions. Of course, times and circumstances change, and we must adjust. But I can't help but believe that our leaders incorporated eternal truths in this organization; it is so evident in the A.N.B. Constitution; and I sometimes wonder if all whom we honor and respect for their leadership abilities in the early days are "rolling over in their graves" when they see what is motivating the minds of our present-day leaders.

Note: The following is a talk I gave to the Alaska Natives Commission several years ago

TESTIMONY BEFORE THE ALASKA NATIVES COMMISSION

November 23, 1992

As Native Americans the problems we are facing are, no doubt, serious ones. However, the dilemmas we are enduring are not only confined to our Native communities—they are universal problems as well. So, as a Native group, when we begin to concentrate on, and solve, those problems that plague us I sincerely believe that we will also be helping to solve the many of the social ills our nation is experiencing as well.

When we embark upon the task of solving our difficulties it is most wise to get to the root of the problem. In many of our quandaries we tend to fix things with band aides—but these repairs, as repeated occurrences have clearly demonstrated, are only temporary ones. Usually the problems will emerge somewhere else and, most likely, in various other forms.

Isn't it much better to get to the root of the problem rather than just treat the symptom?

I have had the opportunity to talk to many people about the ills of our society, and a majority agrees that the genuine problems we are facing today are spiritual and moral ones, and the symptom manifestation of these afflictions come in the form of political, economic, and social issues. With that we tend to presume government should solve our problems for us.[61] I have mentioned before that governments can't create jobs. Prosperous people do. Another great ill of our country is the breakdown of the family unit. When we talk about family values, I believe we identify a father, a mother, and children. We can throw in a cat or a dog if we wish. To expand this nice little circle, we must include grandparents and other extended family members. This band of individuals should be linked together like a chain. Herein lay our strength. This is the true value of a family. At the core, it is incomplete when either one of the parents is absent, or there are no children. The reason for the erosion of the family, I believe, is lack of decent values. It is the responsibility of parents to teach their children proper values. The schools, the churches, synagogues, religious institutions, and other organizations are only helpers to the home.

In our Native cultures the family was the most significant unit in society. For instance, in Tlingit tradition, the uncles were the ones who trained the young men how to be hunters and fishers as well as to endure the harshness of the wilderness. My wife tells about how, as a little girl, she used to go to a tribal house to learn the stories, genealogies of families, history, language and hosts of other things. Here youngsters were trained in the laws and mores of their society and learned to have pride in whom and what they were. Today we realize that the importance of parents in the home is to make a place secure and safe for children; without this foundation children can emerge with many undesirable problems which society will have to deal with

---

[61] *Let's admit this also: it is to a large measure, because of our social predicaments with which we have burdened our government, that our national government has such a huge national debt. Not only are these entitlements a burden, but any additional responsibilities put on the tax payers such as bail-outs of banks, insurance companies, auto industries, and taking money we don't have to stimulate the economy; and so we have to borrow from China, Japan, and other countries that will cause inflation by printing more money that is not backed up by gold, etc. Stimulating the economy through government intervention makes things worse. It is mind boggling to realize that we have a nearly 17 trillion debt that will be put onto our grandchildren to deal with for generations to come. Furthermore, we need to admit that responsibilities ought to be put in their proper perspective.*

in the future. The root of the problem here is in the kind of parents we are. Paraphrasing Andy Rooney from 60 Minutes, "If we want good children, we have to raise good parents." Governments cannot make good parents—that is not the proper role of government. I have heard this statement many times and I embrace it full heartedly, "We cannot legislate morality." Nor can we legislate good parenting.

Neither is the teaching of proper values the role of the schools. Our schools should prepare our children to learn how to earn a proper living while it is the duty of the home to teach one how should live a proper life.

I believe it is in from our parents and religious institutions where we learn proper parenting. That is why my premise is that our problems are spiritual and moral. It is through religious training that we learn the proper way in which to conduct our lives; it is through religious training that we learn the principles of morality.

Alexis de Tocqueville was a French political scientist who made an eighteen-month tour through the United States in the mid 1800's. He was sent by his government to find out why America became such a great nation in such a short period of time. He found his answer when he went into the churches throughout the country. Because of his findings he wrote a book entitled Democracy in America. One interesting statement he made was this: "Religion in America takes no direct part in the government of society, but it must be regarded as the first of their political institutions—" In another part he said that "America is great because America is good. America will cease to be great only when it ceases to be good." Herein is the root of Native American problems. Herein, I am convinced, is the root of America's dire ills.

The proper role of government is conclusively stated in the Declaration of Independence. It identifies the reasons why the colonists broke away from England and tells the reasons why the new government was formed. It states that the role of government is to protect our lives, our liberties and to guarantee our pursuit of happiness. Anything more or less than that is usurpation or oppression. The U.S. Constitution was the instrument formed for the purpose of carrying out the intent of the Declaration of Independence; however, it should be noted that there is a difference between the role of government and the Constitution. Government was instituted for controlling people, while the Constitution is supposed to control government. Thomas Jefferson believed that the Constitution is supposed to keep those people whom we elect to represent us in government from getting into mischief. It tells what our President, our legislature, and our courts can and cannot do. The intent of the Framers of the U.S. Constitution was that the three branches of government were designed to balance and check one another. In our modern times our Presidents have misused the power of Presidential Orders. The 17th Amendment to the Constitution crippled the proper power of the legislature by doing away with the appointment of the Senators by state legislatures and made Senators an elective position by the people. Before the 17th Amendment Senators were appointed by the various state legislatures. Senators were obligated to look after the best interest of their respective states, while, because the representatives were elected by the people from the various states, they were supposed to look after the best interest of the people. These are only a few reasons why our government is no longer serving us properly.

Why don't we take a moment and examine what our government should do to rightfully and effectively assist the American citizenry. I also believe that every American, Native and non-native alike, should embark upon a serious study of our U.S. Constitution and learn, for themselves, what the Framer's real intent was. Maybe as we do this we may get a better perspective of what it is that government should do for us.

1. Perhaps we should look at what the free enterprise system is all about. Realizing that it is the engine that drives the economy, perhaps we could insist that the free enterprise system be allowed to take hold in every faction of American society. Herein is what drives our economy. It is a known fact the private enterprises can do for us the things that need to be done much better and cheaper than government can.

2. We are all interested in cutting our national debt and balancing the federal budget. It would be helpful to learn what the true intent of the "Promote the general welfare" and the "Interstate Commerce" clauses in the Preamble of Constitution was and is. The Founding Fathers bitterly debated these concepts before they penned them into the Constitution, and then cautioned future generations about the dangers of miss-interpretation, and where miss-interpretation could eventually lead us.

3. And what about the Supreme Court? Are we making sure it is interpreting the Constitution and not making legislation through its written decisions?

4. Perhaps we need to make sure the legislature is making the laws based on common sense, rather than listening to the special interest groups and lobbyists. Perhaps we should look at the 17th Amendment with a critical eye and bring back the idea that Senators should be appointed by their state legislatures and begin to properly represent the best interests of their respective states.

5. Perhaps we should make sure the President is carrying out the laws, rather than making legislation through his Proclamations and Executive Orders.

6. We are indeed watchdogs of our government and as watchdogs we should make sure that all the above branches of government begin checking and balancing one another.

7. Perhaps we should examine with a critical eye whether the federal government is really interfering with states' rights. The study should include a discussion about letting the states really serve its citizens. I believe the only time the federal government should interfere is when the issue involves problems on a national scale. States and local governments can best serve from a local level.

8. In the original Constitution, the power to tax was reserved for the states, and then the states were obliged to make their contribution into the federal treasury to handle issues and

problems on a national scale, such as road building between states or the national defense. Perhaps we should look at the issue that the people can be best served by those closest to the issue. Maybe we should examine why our taxes are too high, and why our government is too big.

We live in a country that is blessed. No other nation has risen to such proportions as the United States in such a short period of time, even though Native Americans and blacks were severely mistreated—but the nations successes was because of the way our Constitution was framed, which dictates to us how government should operate with all its checks and balances.

We, as Native Americans, fought long and hard to be recognized as citizens. We accomplished that through blood sweat and tears. We have the Alaska Native Brotherhood to thank for that. I liken the Alaska Native Brotherhood Constitution to the U.S. Constitution in its original form. Article I says that Native people will participate in the civil government from the local, state and national level under the spirit of the Declaration of Independence and the Constitution and laws of the United States. The way that we can attain happiness, which is one of the reasons why our government was set up the way it was, is to participate in government. Our task is to learn all we can about constitutional government and what was the real intent by the Founding Fathers, and then make our contribution to righting wrongs committed against us as citizens. One important idea I learned from the Founding Fathers is that we should not let government do what we, ourselves, would be thrown in jail for. When we make corrections based on correct principles Natural Laws) we will be helping other people as well.

Again, the Declaration of Independence states that the purpose of government is to protect our lives, our liberties and to guarantee us our opportunity to achieve happiness. It also clearly states that when our government no longer accomplishes those ends then we are obliged to abolish or alter that government and start a new one based on those same principles—that is the protection of our lives, liberties and properties. I have said this before—I don't believe things are so bad that we must abolish our government just yet—however we can do a lot toward bringing our country back on the right track by altering[62] it and insisting that governments be put back into their proper constitutional order.

Yes, as Native Americans, we have a lot of problems—but again those problems are not so unusual that they are confined just to our Native communities. They are the same problems other ethnic groups and people of the United States are facing, and when we gather, as Americans, and realize this together, then we can begin to rightly solve the perplexing afflictions of our United States as well.

---

[62] The Liberty Amendment will also correct or course.

ANSCA AND AHE FREE ENTERPRISE SYSTEM

The Alaska Native Land Claims Settlement Bill was passed by the U.S. Congress on December 18, 1971. Since the 1930's our fathers and grandfathers fought long and hard for a fair settlement for the taking of our lands, our identity as Natives, and everything that has made us a separate, distinct people—unique in every way; proud, noble, self-sufficient, independent—a people who did not believe in hand-outs from the government—a people who wanted to be Tlingits, Haida's, Tsimshian's, Athabascan' s, Eskimos, Aleuts, but still not subjected to being identified as a reservation under the Indian Reorganization Act, but a people who wanted to be a part of the American system of government—yet sovereign and distinct as it is guaranteed by the U.S. Constitution. When Congress passed the Land Claims Settlement Bill they put some restrictions on the act. The reason why they restricted the stock of the newly formed corporations was to give the Native people of Alaska a period of time (20 years) to learn how to run our corporations and prepare themselves to compete in the free enterprise system of America. This, in my mind's eye, is what 1991 was all about.

We all know that the competitive market in the American system is very rough. Congress knew that if they were to give us our per-capita settlement and thrust us into the world of competition as individuals that we would never be able to survive. Like so many tragedies that happened to our Native American friends in the south forty-eight, we may have lost our identity shortly after our payments were made. So, Congress did something that would assure us at least a half chance to survive, not only as Natives, but as Americans as well, in a world where one can be made or driven to the ground; Congress wrote into the ANCSA Bill the stipulation that all stock in the corporations would be restricted for a period of twenty years. This meant that we, as Native shareholders of our corporations, would not be able to sell our stock, or use it for security so that creditors would not be able to get hold of our stocks to pay off debts; it would be free from taxation, and because of this our lands would be protected. In every sense we were insulated from the "rat-race" and "do or die" world of the American free enterprise system. For twenty years we were supposed to be trained to learn how to succeed in managing our corporations so that we would not sink so quickly in this cruel world of gluttony and competition.

Now the Alaska Federation of Natives, on behalf of all the Native people of Alaska, submitted eight resolutions to Congress for the purpose of amending the land claims settlement. These amendments address the concerns about keeping Native control over our stocks and corporations; we want to be assured of control so that when 1991 came non-shareholders would not be able to buy our stock and take control of our corporations.

We have a close identification with the land and want to keep it free from taxation—we want to be assured that creditors cannot take our land and stock to pay off individual debts; we want to assure our elderly that they receive benefits for the work that they contributed in winning our battle against the U.S. Government on this issue, and we want to see that Native children born after December 18, 1971 could be included in the benefits of the settlement. In every sense we want to be sure that we retain our close ties with the land—to use it for subsistence purposes so that we can continue being Tlingits, Haida's, Tsimshian's, Eskimos, and Aleuts. These are serious and noble concerns, and I must admire the efforts of our leaders have put into these resolutions. When Congress passed these amendments and the President signed it, we all sighed a sigh of relief; and for good reason.

But what is really happening here? Are we admitting something by working so hard to get these amendments attached to the original bill? Can it disguise our concerns for our land, the elderly and the newbornes? I wonder if there is an unacknowledged bottom line here.

We wanted Congress to amend the ANCSA Bill, so we can continue the restrictions we are presently enjoying because we have not yet learned well the task of running all our corporate affairs, and with 1991 was approaching at a fast pace we were in a panic because we realized that we cannot compete in the free enterprise system of America. We are concerned because in a short time we can lose everything that we have that identifies us as a distinct group of aboriginal people.

OUR GREATNESS IS MEASURED IN PROPORTION TO OUR GOODNESS

Tuesday, November 29, 1994

At the Alaska Native Brotherhood and Sisterhood Convention held in Juneau last month, a resolution was adopted by the body to bring prayer and the study of the bible back into the schools. I have to say, without any reservation, this is a worthy proclamation.

I attended a high school in Michigan for two years, and one of the most memorable things I remember about this experience was the devotions we had every morning before we went to our home rooms. It only lasted fifteen minutes but it comprised of a member of a clergy from various denominations who gave an opening prayer and a short reading of the scriptures. This, in my estimation, correctly started the day for me. It also instilled in my friends a deep abiding faith in God and the enforcement of our spirituality. In our Tlingit culture it was important that we paid homage to our Creator, Yeil (Raven), more so in the olden days. It was routine to offer prayers of thanksgiving every part of our awakening days. When we hunted, fished or gathered we recognized the Creator as the provider of all things. When we were converted to Christianity we were taught to do the same things. As Native Americans and Alaska Natives our people believed in living and abiding by the Natural Laws and Natures God

Kadashan Speaks: The Law of Nature and Nature's God

Many of us are concerned with the direction in which the moral fiber of our society is headed these days. It is heartbreaking to see people, especially our young, waste their lives on alcohol, drugs and crime.

Of course, we all have free choice, but what was the "guiding light" that made America a monumental nation? The explanation lies in the forte in the spirituality of its citizens. In order for us as Americans—even more importantly as Native Americans—to enjoy political prosperity, it is eminent that moral and spiritual principles be an integral part of our daily life. The Founding Fathers of the United States and organizers of the Alaska Native Brotherhood and Sisterhood devotions were to the Christian God; however, I strongly believe that our Creator and the Christian Gods are the same. I think we would find that pretty much the case in all cultures.

Thomas Jefferson, one of the Founding Fathers of this nation, wrote a book called "Works." One interesting statement he made was "God rules in the affairs of men and no nation can survive without realizing that fact." Benjamin Franklin also penned the same phrase in some of his thoughts. Thomas Jefferson also emphasized that our liberties are an endowment from God, and that we cannot be a secure people if we take God out of our lives.

Likewise, the American constitutional system is based upon the recognition of God. People lacking in faith should recognize that God is mentioned in the Declaration of Independence five times. Likewise, when we put our hands over our hearts and recite that portion of the Pledge of Allegiance, "—one nation under God, with liberty and justice for all," we as Americans are admitting that we receive everything from a source mightier than ourselves and that we cannot be successful otherwise. We are recognizing that a creator is the source of correct, perpetual principles, as well as the source of our unalienable rights. An unalienable right is anything that is derived from nature; therefore, it can be construed that anything that comes from the natural world cannot be taken away, repealed or abolished. Another definition is that an unalienable right is a God-given right. From these definitions we can recognize that under this system of government the individual, unalienable right to life, liberty and to the pursuit of happiness doesn't derive themselves from the consent of the majority, but rather from the fact that our civil liberties are God-given. Therefore, an overwhelming majority, or any department or level of government, does not have the prerogative to take these away. If these natural rights are taken away from us, then bad things begin to happen.

When the Founding Fathers sheltered themselves in Constitutional Hall to form a new government, they opened and closed their meetings with prayer, recognizing that they could not be successful in creating a new government without the aid of Providence. When the Alaska Native Brotherhood was being formed the Founders also recognized that God had guided them every day they deliberated on the merits of the organization. I am convinced that deity established the Constitution of this land by the minds and the fingertips of wise men of whom were raised up for that very purpose.

From the Native perspective the Founders of the Alaska Native Brotherhood were, likewise, raised up for furnishing us with an organization that recognized God as the source of our might. The ANB Constitution has eternal principles that ensure us safety and protection if we will exercise these spiritual precepts in our lives.

I think it is imperative that we come to understand these principles because they will save us from the lack of control that challenges our intellect, our sense of right and wrong, our spirituality. The oath of office encourages us to look to God to keep us steadfast, and the preamble in our Constitution challenges us to create a true respect in ourselves, and in other persons with whom we deal, for the "letter and spirit of the Declaration of Independence and for the Constitution and laws of the United States." So, you see the ANB Constitution embraces the spirituality and love of country and patriotism in this organization. When we take the oath of office and membership we promise that "we will look to our Heavenly Father for wisdom and strength to keep you steadfast?"

Our Founders pledged allegiance to the flag and like the Founders of this nation had opening and closing prayers in all their meetings. Because of the belief and faith in Providence and country, the American forefathers were a strong and a steadfast family.

Now we know that much has been debated regarding the separation of church and state in America. I suppose debaters on both sides of the fence will continue to disagree until a legitimate understanding of these institutions is eventually apparent. This issue, however, should be understood that the Founders did not want any one religious sect to dominate the lives of its citizens.[63] Their experiences with King George prompted them to debate this long and hard and they concluded that, even though, religion would play an important part in their daily affairs, that the freedom of choice should be evident to worship whomever or whatever their conscience dictated.

We have learned much by what the early leaders of the nation had to say about this topic. Let us examine one who was not an American. Alexis de Tocqueville was curious as to why America had become a powerful and successful country in such a short period of time.

In his book entitled "Democracy in America" Tocqueville penned a very important concept. He said, "Religion in America takes no direct part in the government of society, but it must be regarded as first of its political institutions." In another place he declared, "Despotism may govern without faith, but liberty cannot. Religion is much more necessary in the republic."

I have said this before, but I really believe that we must realize that the scores of problems we are facing today are not only confined to our Native communities; these are universal problems and the symptomatic manifestations of these quandaries come to us in the form of social, economic and political issues, and so we think that we can solve these problems through government. Can we solve these issues through these avenues when the real roots to these predicaments are moral and spiritual ones?

---

[63] This is what the first amendment to the constitution means

We should realize that the difficulty lies not only in the treatment of the symptoms; to permanently fix something isn't it necessary to get to the root of the problem? Isn't it much more important to attack the cause rather than only treat the symptom?

After Tocqueville completed his visit through the Americas he discovered the secret of America's success. He recognized this important standard after he visited the churches throughout the country. In his book he wrote: "America is great because America is good. America will cease to be great only when it ceases to be good."

And so, it is with us Native Americans and Alaska Natives. We are; indeed, stately citizens and we can be statelier yet, but our greatness can only be measured in proportion to our goodness.

I believe this resolution is a good one. I believe, more than what the contemporary politicians are promising us these days that we need a restoration of old and proven values rather than any kind of reformation. May we follow the fine examples already set forth by the Founders of this great country and the early leaders of Alaska Native Brotherhood and Sisterhood. We can help set the standard not only for ourselves, but our example can set the stage for the entire nation as well.

THREE TLINGITS AND A GENIE

February 21, 1995

One of our prestigious leaders, Roger Lang, who has since gone to the *spirit world of the Tlingits*, made a timely statement at an Alaska Native Brotherhood Convention at Sitka several years ago, which proved to be a very momentous expletive to me. He said, "1991 is approaching at a rapid pace, and we can't stop it."

    It was only a few short years ago that these apprehensive words came from the core of his heart and now 1991 has come and gone. Many of our people are gravely concerned because of the trepidation that we, as natives, have a chance of losing all we have because of the free enterprise system in America. When 1991 came upon us the restrictions that were placed on the Alaska Native Settlement Claims Act (ANSCA) would have been lifted. When ANSCA was instigated, Congress made a stipulation in the bill that the corporations that will be formed would not be able to sell the stocks for a period of twenty years. The rationale was that this would give amble time for rising, young leaders to learn how to run for-profit corporations and compete in the corporate world. Twenty years to learn how to run a for-profit corporation is very generous. Some people jump into the corporate world in a day and either sink or swim overnight, while others are trained through leadership of family or friends; they too could either fail or become strong influences in the corporate world. The fear for us, however, is that if we are forced into the system we may not only lose

KADASHAN SPEAKS: THE LAW OF NATURE AND NATURE'S GOD

what we have materially but, more importantly, our identity as Alaskan Natives. With this reality facing us, some people think it would have been better if things had remained the way they had been for Natives in the years gone by. Some of these selected leaders are striving to locate find, some shareholders are indifferent, while others aren't sure how to instruct their leaders.[64]

At the same convention someone told a story about three Tlingits and a genie. He told it as a humorous story; everyone laughed and applauded but I have since thought it over and have come up with an interpretation that I thought is appropriate for this particular yarn.

It appears that three Tlingits were walking along the ocean beach where they came upon a peculiar bottle. One of the Tlingits picked up the bottle and removed the cap.

Pop! Out comes a dark, funny man dressed in silky, colorful clothing. He had a cloth that seemed twirled around his head.

"Greetings to you." He said. "I've been trapped in that prison for hundreds of years. Because you were responsible for freeing me I have the power to grant you three wishes."

Then he said to one of the Tlingits, "What is your wish?"

"I wish," said the first Tlingit, "that I had a lot of money." Swish, boom, bang! In an instant his wish was granted.

Turning to one of the other Tlingits the Genie asked, "And what shall be your wish be?"

"I wish I had a new home, a new car, and all the comforts of the world," was his answer. Swish, boom, bang! In an instant his wish was granted.

Evidently the wishes had transferred the two Tlingits to another place because the third Tlingit suddenly found that he was alone.

"What wish my I have the pleasure of granting you?" the Genie asked of him.

This Tlingit realized something: he missed his friends very much.

---

[64] With this kind of uncertainty in our Tlingit society I think it is absolutely necessary to return to the Natural Laws.

Kadashan Speaks: The Law of Nature and Nature's God

"I wish my friends were back here with me," he said. In an instant his wish was granted.

Let's assume now that these three Tlingits lived before the Alaska Native Land Claims Settlement Act came into being. In those days they lived a satisfying life; they practiced their traditions, they cherished their culture and enjoyed their subsistence way of life.

Now the bottle symbolized the land claims settlement and the Genie what the settlement had to offer: their riches which would replace the subsistence lifestyle, a new home and car—all the comforts of life that the Anglo-Saxon influence brought, anything that threatened to erase their culture and tradition.

That famous statement we have all heard one time or another: "Be careful of what you wish for—you just might get it" evidenced itself: the money, the car, the new home was very attractive to two of the Tlingits, for they wished these upon themselves and got what they wished for.

These two Tlingits symbolize those who got caught up in the land claims settlement, while the third Tlingit symbolizes those who were left behind. These could be the elders and those who understood what is the most valuable in their lives: the land and what it, at one time, provided for our people, and their subsistence life-style. He was the one who was able to see what was happening to the other two Tlingits, and his wish was that the things were back to the way they used to be. Many of us feel that way now, don't we?

Yes, 1991 has come and gone, and as Roger Lang said, "We couldn't stop it."

But neither can we go back to the way it used to be for our people.[65] Almost overnight a group of us have been thrust into the corporate world while yet another, younger group have been left out. These are serious problems and concerns that we are being faced with now, and they are certainly affecting every true-blooded Alaskan to the fullest.

Finally, I appreciated another thing that Roger Lang said that day during the ANB Convention in Sitka. He said something to the affect

---

[65] However—please see Sometimes We Need to Go Back to move forward.

that even though 1991 is coming and that there is nothing we can do about it, "It will not stop Alaska Natives from being Alaska Natives"

I liked that. I know it is true. After all, there are Italians, Irish, Mexicans, Chinese, Scandinavians and all races of people in America, and they are all allowed to enjoy their own and various kinds of foods, practice their religion, culture and traditions. Yet, they remain a very distinct and proud people. After all they, and we, are Americans.

The one advantage that we have overall is that we were the very first ones, and because of this we have been conveyed upon us a very good and proud advantage and heritage, indeed.

HOME, THE CENTER OF ALL LIVING

December 6, 2002

I was saddened and alarmed by the recent articles in the Empire about the problems with drugs in Juneau. This problem is prevalent in our small villages as well.

A long time ago one of our children barged into the house after school. "Hi mom." I'm home."

But mom wasn't there. Instead she was hanging clothes on a clothes line in the back yard to dry in the brisk, spring breeze. When she came into the house she found a weeping lad sitting on the front porch.

"What's wrong, son?"

"Nothing," he sobbed. "You just weren't here when I came home.

There's this touching scene in a movie. A father was comforting his daughter after she was attacked in a secluded area while she was walking home from school. "I called for you," she said. "I called for you and you didn't come."

What profound statements!

I have witnessed over the past couple of decades a strong drive to subsidize programs in the schools that attempt to do what really should be taking place in the home. I have also witnessed grant funds used to bring education about the ills of drug and alcohol into the schools. The fine work went well in the schools, but the most important place was never outreached: the home. I have always said in discussions about the problems we have that we can bring a host of programs through grants in the schools to attempt to educate our children about the evils of alcohol and drugs. But if we don't reach inside the home, all is for naught. A child can partake of all these programs and he or she can learn about the ills of these, but at the end of the school day—when they come back home and find their parent or parents high on alcohol or drugs or are abusive then all that they have learned that day will do down the drain—so to speak.

Several years ago, I attended a Head Start Conference in Washington DC. I listened to speakers talk about how our President and his wife were instigating policies to place more responsibility on community action groups, etc. The theme was "It takes a village (community) to raise a family." While this is true, I really don't believe the bona fide responsibility should be usurped from the head and heart of the home: parents.

In the olden days it was in Tlingit culture that children were trained by the aunts and uncles and elders in the village. When boys turned eight years old they were given to the uncle. The uncles had been trained by their uncles who had been trained by their uncles, etc., according to the Natural Laws. It was the uncle's responsibility to begin teaching the youngsters how to survive in the wilderness and to hunt and fish. The discipline was harsh, but necessary if the boys were going to grow up to be a productive member of the village. One way to toughen the youngster was to have him bath in cold sea water every day during the four seasons. This was to toughen the boy so that when the real test was to come he would be able to endure the challenging times in the wilderness while he hunted and fished for his family and the community. To be able to survive in the wilderness one had to learn to abide by the laws of nature.[66]

The same pattern was done with the girls although they were not required to soak in cold sea water.

---

[66] In a future book I will share personal stories about how this discipline helped me through life threatening events. There were many and of course will take a book to relate them

In the evenings youngster would go to a tribal house where an elder would tell creation stories, histories and demonstrate importance of culture, song and dance. When the young men reached puberty he was sent along with his elders on long journeys when trading expeditions were done. Sometimes it may take months and years to go on such a trip, but this was also important because the young men learned histories, traditions, song and dances of other peoples. "It is just like us sending our young people away to college today," an elder said recently. "When he returns home, he is ready to be of service to his village either as a leader or proficient hunter and provider"

This practice was done away with when the government and missionaries came and tried to assimilate our people into the western society. The balance in the lives of these people was no longer there and today we have a lot of Native people looking for themselves. Not knowing who you are is devastating to an individual and it can cause many problems that can take one down the wrong trails into villages that are strange to the well-being of a group of people who thrived and survived off the land.

Today we must put our lives into proper perspective and the parents must take on the responsibility those uncles, aunts and grandparents had in the past. Today the head of the home should be the father. It is he who provides leadership and stability in the home. It is he who works and provides the food and shelter for his family. The wife, on the other hand, is the heart. It is she who gives the children the sense of security by nurturing love and understanding. Without the head and the heart, we have a dysfunctional family—a social ill that is very difficult to correct once it is set free to spread.

We have seen during this same couple of decades the gradual breakdown of the family unit. We seem to think other people, or institutions, should do what we don't want to do ourselves. It is true, in the American systems, we can delegate to government and other institutions, things that we cannot do for ourselves; stuff like police protection, transportation and education. But being a parent cannot, in anyway, be delegated to the schools, churches or other entities like we see in many communities today; we can never be freed from being parents. This is a responsibility we took upon ourselves when we entered the covenant of marriage and began to populate our communities.

After my wife and I devoted our energies to raising eight children, we are now watching them raise their own families. One of our daughters has a full-time job. Indeed, it requires both her and her husband to work to adequately provide for themselves and their two children. But they have never delegated raising their children to anyone else other than immediate family. The children are well rounded and never with need of food, shelter, clothing—or love. These kids are learning responsibility and we are witnessing how they grew up and raising their families much like they were raised. Our youngest son has been married for thirteen years now—they have two beautiful daughters and three sons. My daughter-in-law told me that she wanted a large family— fourteen children to be exact— and that she is committed to being a "stay-at-home-mom." Bless her soul. Robert has a good job but he also has the talent and capacity to take on part time work and both jobs seem to keep them very well—and he still has time to spend quality time with his wife and children. I do know that those fourteen children will have an excellent chance of surviving. These are only examples of how the rest of our family is following this procedure of raising their own off-spring. Today my wife and I have over thirty grandchildren and half a dozen great grandchildren, and they have all made us proud.

One of our sons made a statement I thought was significant and, yet, very frightening. He said, "If you send your children to day care centers, when you grow old they will put you in an old people's home." In the olden days families took care of their children, and when they grew into the sunset of their years the children and grandchildren took watched over their parents and grandparents.

I am reminded often about a concept Andy Rooney expressed during one of his commentaries at the end of the CBS television program 60 Minutes. He said, "If we want good children we are going to have to raise good parents." Indeed, herein is the root of many of our problems in our social order today.

Well, I believe good parents are parents who are willing to set the proper example for their children. They have that responsibility at the least. If you don't want your children to smoke or use tobacco, consume alcohol, or use drugs—then don't do it yourselves; then if you ever have to council your children on these problems, it will mean more to them when you can say, "Don't do as I say. Do as I do."

BACK TO THE BASICS— OUR RIGHTS

July 23, 2010

Part One

I am responding to a recent Empire composition by one Evon Peter that was forwarded to me in an email. While I agree that his words are well spoken, and also agree that they should be carefully examined so that we can make an informed decision when we go to the voting booths this fall. I have been watching closely the advertisements exposed to us from both sides of the campaigns and I am not sure that they are helping me make an informed decision. The real issue here was expressed in my previous article, **The Spectrum of the Constitutional Eagle**, and I trust that my readers were able to get the message of whether we want more government influencing our lives— or do we want less?

Many good things have happened to advance Alaska Native issues regarding human rights. Let's remember the early leaders of the Alaska Native Brotherhood and how they brainstormed a vision to advance our people to be among the most cultivated in the world. The crusade began way back in 1912 when they organized the Alaska Native Brotherhood and labored long and hard to be recognized as citizens. Look on the back of the ANB membership cards and review, if you will, the 15 points of accomplishments they gained for all Alaska Natives. Many of our early leaders have given their blood, sweat and tears to prove this. Read the first essay in this book entitled **One of The First**.[67] Here you will learn about my firsthand experience with Roy and Elizabeth Peratrovich and their effort to integrate the school systems in Juneau; but the most intriguing was Sister Peratrovich's discourse to the Territorial Legislature condemning discrimination. All Alaskans benefited from her powerful speech which changed Alaska for the better. Long before there was a Martin Luther King, there was an Elizabeth Peratrovich.

Did you know when this country was being formed that it was the intent to include Native Americans as the Fourteenth Colony? In the epilogue in this work **Reclaiming Our Power** you will learn more about this and why it didn't happen. In a nutshell there were a series of policies the federal government instigated to address Indian issues from assimilation to extermination to Indian Reorganization and relocation to Self-Determination and Self-Governance. Each one was a process that enabled Native Americans to take more and more responsibilities for their own destinies. Let me say that the Self-Governance Demonstration Project started way back in the Reagan Administration and that it was John McCain who co-sponsored the bill. Because of the passage of this legislation many Tribal Governments have been able to take a good portion of these programs, functions, service and activities from the Bureau of Indian Affairs (BIA) and administer the essential programs themselves. Notwithstanding the fact that there are still many problems we encounter daily; tribal leaders have risen to the occasion many times— and prevailed.

Sure, our people's lands have been exploited and many people were put on reservations, but for those who did not want to live on reservations the Native Allotment Act of 1906 was passed by Congress. This gave people the opportunity to own up to 160 acres of their own land and to develop it—agreed that even these were exploited by non-natives however, in many instances; we let it happen to ourselves. The BIA let many Natives in Alaska have restricted deeds to lands for their own purpose and advancement. I know several people who had businesses in their homes in Yakutat and profited well from it.

---

[67] Page 120 in this work

Many Founders of the Alaska Native Brotherhood were, indeed, sent to boarding schools. The reason was that their parents wanted them to be educated so they can gain their rights to citizenship, effectively fight segregation and discrimination, and learn to cope with the pressures of a cash economy. When the Indian Reorganization Act (IRA) was passed in 1934 this applied to reservations in the south 48 only. Save for the Metlakatla Reserve, Alaska had no reservations. When our young, future, leaders were attending boarding schools in the south 48 they saw, first hand, the adverse conditions on reservations and came home dead set against the reservation idea. In 1936 the act was amended to include Alaska without the reservation requirement. In the mid 1940's there were long, bitter, debates on the floors of the Alaska Native Brotherhood Conventions that nearly drowned the organization. The initial requirement was that if a community wanted to take advantage of the IRA they had to request reservation status. The schism was about half and half among the members, but when the membership realized what it was happening to the organization they decided on a compromise. If a community wanted an IRA, the ANB would assist in helping them achieve it—however they were not going to force it on anyone either.

The ANB and ANS have always been strong promoting education; in recent years we have seen a consorted effort among our people to bring back our language, song, dance, and traditions. Because Native peoples had no reservations there, of course, were no treaties between IRA's and the federal government to enforce. We were citizens and the treaty we have with the federal government is the Constitution of the United State, which allows us the right be to self-governing. Self-governance is a Natural Law and like freedom, must be fought for every day in the political arena.

"Kill the Indian Save the Man" policy was brought in by President Andrew Jackson. He was an old Indian fighter and his administration enforced his extermination policy. Of course, after all the damage was done the Howard Wheeler Act—or as we know it today as the Indian

Reorganization Act—finally gave Indians the opportunity to take more control over their lives.

As for this issue of being able to participate in any form of "their" government, there is this inspiring clause in the Preamble of the ANB Constitution which emphasizes that we will involve ourselves "in the civil government of Alaska under the spirit of the Declaration of Independence and the Constitution and laws of the United States." This challenge for Native Alaskans has taken us leaps and bounds forward since then. Many of our communities in Alaska are administered by their own Native people. Tribal governments are also becoming very powerful in the villages.

Because we are citizens of the United States Natives are governed under the State of Alaska laws. We have just as much rights as any other citizen. Warranted that there is, indeed, still a lot of prejudice in our society especially in the schools in the urban communities., the standard has been established by our forefathers that we must constantly campaign for.

That is our right—!

It is our duty!

So many times we let things happen to us and I have always proclaimed that we should not allow this—let's stand up and scrap for those rights that have been given us by the Creator and the Constitution of the United States. Oh yes, the Alaska Constitution pretty much mirrors the federal one too. The tools are there—let's use them to our benefit.

I realize that I have addressed only a few issues that Mr. Peters is concerned with. I try my best not to keep my compositions too long, so I'll reserve those for the next issue. Stay tuned.

BACK TO THE BASICS—OUR RIGHTS

July 30, 2009

Part Two

One of my readers responded to a previous article[68] about how we can address issues, problems and concerns by abiding by basic principles; he agreed that "we have the tools" to address our many problems, and he challenged: "Let's use them." We can never win over issues safe guarding our life-styles unless we use the tools that are available to us. Although administrative policies may make it difficult to have things our way, we must be diligent in our effort to see that honorable laws are carried out. These tools are, of course, the U.S. and State Constitutions and the rule of law that are based from the Natural Law and God's Law.

The Declaration of Independence mandates that we are all endowed by the Creator with certain unalienable rights; such rights are the protection of our lives, our liberties, and our pursuit of happiness. I think most everyone understands the clause in the Declaration that assures us the protection of our lives and liberties; however, the broadness of the pursuit of happiness idea may be confusing.

The Founders believed that our governments should guarantee us the right to pursue happiness. They also believed our pursuit should

---

[68] Back to Basics, Part one.

be in whichever way we want so long as we do not interfere with the right of others to do the same, but I think the basic reason was that we should have the right to provide for our families the ABC's of survival. To accomplish this we need to be assured we have shelter, clothing and food— and to be kept safe from harm. This also means that we should be guaranteed ways and means of survival so these things can be provided for us. This is where the idea of a cash economy enters our lives—meaning that the ways and means of survival ensures that we have adequate income by having the right to engage in whatever occupation we desire. Another thing that we should be assured of is that we, as Native peoples, can survive off our lands and resources; this is what I like to refer to as a **land-based economy** where we can subsist off the resources of the land. These are natural rights that cannot be taken from us because they are derived from Nature or, as many people would embrace, are given us by the Creator. Despite the broadness of the Declaration on this matter, it is clear what the Founders meant by this statement.

The Alaska National Interest Lands Conservation Act (ANILCA) was designed to allow us to live off a **land-based economy**, however there was long and hard discussion in the Congress as to whether it should be a <u>Native</u> privilege only. The equal access issue was seriously debated because the Declaration of Independence and the United States Constitution says that that we are all equal and should have the same rights to use the resources as anyone else. In the end Congress decided that it would insert <u>rural </u>rather than Native in the act. That's what we must live with today, and it is one of the reasons why the State and Federal systems are constantly at odds with each other.[69] Another issue at odds between the state and feds is the rural preference ideology as identified in ANILCA. Section 801 clearly states that rural and Native people can participate in a land-based economy (subsistence activities) if they are qualified, however it recognizes that subsistence by Natives is essential for their physical, traditional, economic, and social existence. The same is said about non-native people, but the State's position is that

---

[69] In a future article I'll try and address State's Rights issues.

these are in direct conflict with the State Constitution which says in Article VIII, Section 1:

"It is the policy of the State to encourage the settlement of its land and the development of its resources by making them available to maximum use consistent with the public interest."

Section 2 also says: "The legislature shall provide for the utilization, development and conservation of all-natural resources belonging to the State, including land and waters, for the maximum benefit of its people."

These two clauses in the States' Constitution is why the State of Alaska backed itself out of compliance with ANILCA and refused to support the rural preference directive mandated in the law of the land. This happened a couple of administrations ago and a lawsuit or two has made it difficult for the state to come back into compliance, even if it wanted to, until these litigations are settled. Even though the state constitutional policy says that all people will benefit from its natural resources and the state will assure that lands, water, and resources will be developed for the benefit of all people, ANILCA does, under federal law, provide a subsistence priority for Natives living in rural areas, and the regulations allows us to use our traditional and cultural knowledge to take fish and wildlife resources on federal lands. Prior to ANILCA the State had subsistence regulations and when ANILCA was passed this became the law of the land. ANLCA also gave the State of Alaska subsistence management authority, however it mandated that it must be administered under federal laws, however the State still has jurisdiction over their own and private lands. ANILCA is, of course, the law of the land, and so the State violated the law when it went out of compliance.

There's another interesting provision in ANILCA worth looking at. Section 807 spells out a procedure where an individual, or organization, can file a civil action against the federal or state government whenever either one or both deviate from Section 805, which speaks to the rural preference provision. It says that when all possible efforts have been made to compel the entity to come into compliance the court would require that the entity will develop regulations to provide for a priority.

So, when we see an issue that confronts us and gives us serious concern, we should look at what is already on the books to address the problem rather than trying to instigate new regulations. When we see fit to make new regulations or laws, let's base it on the State and Federal Constitutions so that we do not go too far astray from the concept of just laws to guide us in our traditional life-styles. It is our right—it is our duty—to be the watch-dogs of the governments' ability to provide laws to our advantage. The Declaration of Independence clearly states that governments are instituted for the purpose of safe-guarding our natural right to life, liberty and pursuit of happiness[70] and we should be grateful for that.

---

[70] In Gregory Schaaf's book Wampum Belts And Peace Trees we learn that the pursuit of happiness idea came from the Native Americans

SOMETIMES WE NEED TO GO BACK TO MOVE FORWARD

Sunday, October 13, 2002

I have been giving some serious thought about candidates convincing voters that their manifesto is the one that will be healthier for Alaska. We have individuals, and special interest groups, who think a candidate is the one whom we should vote for because that particular character will do such and such for our benefit. We've had proponents who want to keep the capital where it is—others would like it moved. We are caught into the idea of providing more opportunities for economic development; the issue of opening ANWR for oil development and invading the Permanent Fund to close the budget gap are stands we also get wedged into. I have even read about folk's crossing over party lines to promote the election of an individual. And then we have this candidate, we think, is best for Native interests. While all of these are of importance to me, I have yet to hear an aspirant address what the real purpose of government is. Yes, I believe that we should be aware of what governments, whether it is local, tribal, state or federal, should be doing for us.

Check out the Declaration of Independence if you will. It outlines clearly what the Founders have commissioned regarding the role of government. It says that this government was instituted for the purpose of protecting us.

Protecting what?

Why protecting our lives, our liberties and guaranteeing our pursuit of happiness.

So what does this idea of protecting our lives involve? We should be able to enjoy the freedom to live wherever and however we want without the fear of having our lives and properties threatened or taken from us. Our children should be able to go to school, we should be able to go work, and our families should be able to enjoy life without being shot at. We should be able to protect ourselves to a certain extent, but if we are unable to elect good people to do for us what we cannot do for ourselves.

What about this liberty thing? The Founders believed that we should be able to do anything with our lives so long as we do not interfere with the rights of others to do the same thing. Native Americans practiced this principle as well. We have the right to say what we want to say.

The other day I had the misfortune of listening to someone who said things that I did not agree with. "Man!" I said to myself, "Do I want to fight to the death on his behalf for his right to say that?"

And what about this issue of being able to worship whomever or whatever we desire?

And then, of course, there's that other stuff the Bill of Rights spells out. What a country!

Now what about the pursuit of happiness part? Here's something interesting—the Founders debated about using the word property in place of happiness, but many of the framers had slaves, who were regarded as property and to escape embarrassment they decide to use the phrase pursuit of happiness instead. So, let's now analyze the phrase so we can better understand it.

To be happy we should have the right to provide for our basic needs and for our families. This means, in these days, we should have a good education so that we can secure a decent job whereby our basic wants can be satisfied: food, shelter, and clothing. Fulfilling these necessary needs helps us to concentrate on other types of advancement that will make our lives much richer and meaningful. To fulfill these obligations one would have to have the ability to earn a wage, which means he works for someone or owns a business. In either case ownership of property must be sanctioned to achieve happiness through these means.

So, as I read it, governments are instituted for the purpose of protecting our lives, our liberties, and guaranteeing ways in which we can enjoy happiness. The declaration also states that when our government no longer does these—that is protect our lives, our liberties, and our pursuit of happiness, then it is our right, it is our duty as Americans, to either alter or abolish our present government and then start a new one that is based upon those same principles. You have heard me say this repeatedly and I have to say that this is a principle that many of us need to learn and use as a mechanism to change things when we are unsatisfied. Now, I don't believe we need to abolish our governments yet, however there is a lot of altering we can do.

Well, one great person I admire said something profound that I think applies here. He said, "Sometimes it is necessary for us to go back if we want to move forward." I think it's time we returned to proven principles if we want a reliable understanding of what governments should really be doing for us.

MANAGEMENT OF RESOURCES OR MANAGEMENT OF PEOPLE

Tuesday, March 29, 1994

Thirteen fishermen from Yakutat, Alaska have been anxiously awaiting a final decision from Alaska Superior Court Judge Jahnke regarding a discrimination issue which they won in a trial against the State of Alaska's Department of Fish and Game, the Alaska Board of Fisheries, and the State of Alaska.

This issue dates back thirteen years ago when surf fishing was closed for periods of time on the Alsek and East Alsek Rivers. The real conflict was between the Native and non-native fishermen, refereed by a fisheries technician, Alex Brogel, an employee for the State of Alaska's Department of Fish and Game.

In the East Alsek River there are two categories of commercial set-netting, the "inside" or "in-river", and the "outside, "or "in the breakers" fishing. Traditionally the non-native worked inside the rivers while a majority of Natives set their gear in the surf. These fishermen use skiffs and powerful outboard motors to navigate the river mouths in between the breakers. This type of fishing is unduly hazardous as storms will sometimes discourage the fishermen from setting their gear in the breakers. In the early 1980's the non-native fishermen, backed by processors, drove the Natives downriver from where the better sets were. As a result more and more Native fishermen began to set their gear on the outside of the rivers. When storms drove them inside, competition for sets became bitter between Native and non-native fishers. It got to the point where fist fights ensued and even gun shots from the white fishermen were fired at Native tents and into their skiffs.

In the 1960's Alex Brogel came onto the scene as a fisheries technician for the State of Alaska. He developed a reputation as an influencer of emergency orders which favored the non-native fishermen. He also made derogatory remarks about Natives and wasn't bashful about making contemptuous slurs about Native women.

When fishing wasn't productive and fishing time diminished in the Situk and Ahrnklin Rivers Native fishermen began to run their skiffs the 50 miles from Yakutat to the Alsek and East Alsek Rivers. When the rivers became too crowded Native fishermen started setting their nets in the surf in areas where the salmon would mill before entering the river. The complaint non-native fishers had was that the surf fishing intercepted salmon that would normally be caught in-river. Records, however, show that this wasn't so. Studies reveal that the harvest was 60:40 percent in favor of the in-river people. From the years between 1980 to 1983 Brogel regulated the opening and closing of the fishing to increasingly favor the non-natives. By emergency-order he closed the surf fishing and kept the in-river opened.

On July 7, 1980 Walter Johnson, one of the plaintiffs in this case, filed a complaint with the Human Rights Commission alleging that the surf fishermen were discriminated against on the account of race, in violation of AS 18.80.255 (1). On January 21, 1983 the Human Rights Commission ruled in favor of the surf fishermen and ordered the Department of Fish and Game and the Alaska Board of Fisheries to be "enjoined from issuing and/or enforcing any regulation, order, or other official measure closing the surf at the Alsek or East Rivers at times when fishing within these rivers is allowed" (Alaska State Commission For Human Rights, Docket No. S 80-0707-159-G).

After the bench trial on May 3, 1988 the Superior Court for the state of Alaska came out with a Memorandum of Decision (No.1JU-85-2764-Civil) in compliance with the Human Rights Commission's findings entitling the plaintiffs to declaratory relief, alleging that "the regulations and emergency orders were implemented and enforced from 1980-1983 without mechanisms to insure plaintiffs access to in-river fishing areas, thereby impairing plaintiffs access." However, the court decided that there was no convincing evidence to show that access was impaired after 1983, therefore no injunctive relief for lost profits was necessary. The plaintiffs won the right and access to surf fishing and proved in the bench trial through Brogel s actions and comments that they were clearly discriminated against because of race, but the court (Judge Jahnke) would not award them punitive damages.

Plaintiffs appealed and on November 29, 1991 the Supreme Court issued an order for a new trial. The court found judgment as affirmed in part, reversed in part, and modified in part and the case was remanded for a re-determination of damages. Here it appeared that plaintiffs would be awarded punitive damages, and the Superior Court was to decide as to amount, etc.

On March 24, 1993 Superior Court Judge Jahnke issued a Memorandum of Decision and Order on Remand. Again, the decision states that plaintiffs were entitled to declaratory damages but not compensation for punitive damages. The reasoning was that the State claimed sovereign immunity, which included the State's immunity from punitive damages. However, it brought out the fact that plaintiffs could be awarded damages if they proved they suffered mental anguish.

One of the Plaintiffs claimed that he did, indeed, suffer mental anguish, and the court calculated that he would be entitled to $ 5,000.00 in damages, however the other plaintiffs did not make this claim therefore no monetary damages was to be awarded the rest of the surf fishermen.

In an interview with eight of the surf fishermen mentioned as plaintiffs in the lawsuit the question was posed to them: "You have won your right to surf fish, now what gives you the right to be compensated?"

One answer was thirteen years of waiting for this issue of discrimination to be brought out into the open. But the most important factor was that the State of Alaska's Department of Fish and Game must be reprimanded so that this kind of thing cannot happen again.

"I have been a police officer for 31 year," says Joe Malatesta, who works for plaintiff's attorney as an investigator. "This is the most interesting, yet the saddest case I've ever worked on in my entire life! When I started investigating this case," he said, "I went through seven or eight boxes of material. When I read some of that stuff I went outside and puked when I read what the state did to these guys."

Brogel is now retired and lives in Skagway, Alaska with full state benefits. The other fish and game officials mentioned as defendants in the lawsuit have not been reprimanded; in fact, they have been promoted one way or another in the department.

On October 13, 1993 Judge Jahnke not only upheld the previous judgment but ruled that plaintiffs pay the states court and attorney fee amounting to $ 39,759.72. The case was appealed, once again, to the Alaska Supreme Court, which plaintiffs will have to post bond in the mount equal to the judgment.

In the words of Arthur S. Robinson, attorney for Plaintiffs, "First, the state discriminates against the Natives based on race, and then the court refuses to award them their just compensation. Now the state wants to be paid for its unlawful conduct."

RELIGION IN AMERICA

Many of us are concerned with the direction in which the moral fiber of society is focused these days. Many are troubled when we see our friends, neighbors, and even in which our own family members are heading. It is sad to see our young people waste their lives on alcohol, drugs, free love, and crime. Many of us have gone down that trail ourselves. We know what this kind of living is like. It is evident that today's society has drifted from a principle of life the elders in our communities treasured so dearly. Of course, we all have free choice, but what was the "guiding light" which made America monumental?

The answer lies in our spirituality. In order for us as American citizens—even more importantly as Native Americans—to enjoy political prosperity it is meaningful that moral and spiritual principles be an indispensable support in our daily living.

Thomas Jefferson, one of the Founding Fathers of this Nation, wrote a book called *Works*. One interesting statement he made was, "God rules in the affairs of men and no nation can survive without realizing this fact." He also emphasized that our liberties are a gift from God and we cannot be a secure people if we take God out of our lives.

Likewise, the American constitutional system is based on the recognition of God. When we put our hands over our hearts and recite that part of the Pledge of Allegiance,"—one nation under God, with liberty and justice for all—" we are admitting, that we receive everything from a source mightier than ourselves, and that we cannot be successful otherwise. We are recognizing the fact that God is the source of correct, eternal principles of government, and also the source of our unalienable rights. From this we recognize that under this system of government individual unalienable right to <u>life</u>, <u>liberty</u>, and the <u>pursuit of happiness</u> does not derive itself from the consent of the majority, but rather from the certainty that these rights are God-given; therefore an overwhelming majority, or department of government, does not have the authority to take these away.

When the Founding Fathers locked themselves in Constitutional Hall to form a new government, they opened and closed their meetings with prayer, knowing full well they would not be successful in creating a new government without the aid of Providence. I am convinced that Deity established the Constitution of this land by the minds of wise men that were raised up for that very purpose.

The Founding Fathers of the Alaska Native Brotherhood were, likewise, raised up for the very purpose of giving us an organization which recognized God as the source of all our power. Our A.N.B. Constitution has eternal principles which will ensure us safety and protection if we will exercise these precepts in our lives. It is imperative we come to understand these principles because they will save us from the ills in our lives which will challenge our intelligence, our sense of right and wrong, our spirituality. The oath of office encourages us to look to God to keep us steadfast, and the preamble in our constitution tells us that we must create a true respect in ourselves, and in other persons with whom we deal, for the "letter and spirit of the Declaration of Independence and for the Constitution and laws of the United States." Our Founding Fathers pledged allegiance to the flag and had opening and closing prayers in all their meetings. Because of the belief and faith in Providence and Country, our forefathers were a strong and steadfast people.

Now we know that much has been debated regarding the separation of Church and State in America. I suppose debaters on both sides of the fence will continue to disagree until a legitimate understanding of these institutions is eventually apparent.

We can learn much by what the early leaders of the nation had to say. Let us examine one who was not an American. His name was Alexis de Tocqueville, a French economist and political scientist. He was curious as to why America had become such a powerful and successful country in such a short period of time. In the mid 1800's he made an eighteen-month tour throughout America. After his visit he wrote a two-volume book entitled <u>Democracy in America</u>. In it he wrote a very important concept: "Religion in America takes no direct part in the government of society, but it must be regarded as first of their political institutions." In another place he declared, "Despotism may govern without faith, but liberty cannot. Religion is much more necessary in the republic."

Now the many problems we are facing today are not only confined to our Native communities; these are universal problems and the symptom manifestation of these quandaries come to us in the form of social, economic, and political issues. However, the real roots to these predicaments are actually moral and spiritual. The difficulty lies only in the treatment of the symptoms. To permanently fix something, isn't it necessary to get to the root of the problem? Isn't it much more important to attack the cause, rather than only treat the symptom?

After Alexis de Tocqueville completed his visit through America he discovered the secret of America's success. He recognized this important standard after he visited the churches in the country. In his book he wrote, "America is great because America is good. America will cease to be great only when it ceases to be good."

And so it is with us as Native Americans and Alaska Natives. We can be greater. But our greatness will only be measured in proportion to our goodness.

May we follow the fine examples already set forth by the Founders of these great and good organizations, the Alaska Native Brotherhood and Sisterhood. We can help set the standard, not only for ourselves, but for the whole nation as well.

PEACE AND PROSPERITY REQUIRES FREEDOM, BASED ON NATURAL LAW

Monday, July 27, 2009

In this day and age, I believe the most important issues we ought to be concerned with are rooted upon some very basic human values—principles that are based upon what too many people are not familiar with these days: The Natural Law. The principle of freedom is based upon a Natural Law. Natural Law is something that is derived from the Creator or is emerged from nature which, if we want to attach this to our everyday living, is "right reasoning" or for a better definition is called wisdom and if used in is government justice. Right reasoning today is, indeed, needed in the way our governments operate these days. Our Founders had it and used their combined wisdom to bring forth a constitution that was to be an envy of the world. We humans, to maintain happiness in our lives, crave for peace and prosperity. The Founders also knew that if prosperity and peace were to abound that they would have to have freedom. History has a habit of repeating itself, and history has repeatedly shown that when freedom fails famine invariably follows. The reason why freedom and liberty fail are because people will take their nations against the Natural Laws.

Several years ago I attended an International Halibut Commission meeting in Anchorage, Alaska. As I listened to testimonies about allocation, conservation and enhancing the resources I was reminded about an article I read in U.S. News and World Report several years ago entitled "10 Billion for Dinner, Please." The article emphasized that this earth can produce for a population of at least 80 billion people—eight times the 10 billion expected to inhabit the earth by 2050! Another study estimates that with improved scientific methods the earth could feed as many as one thousand billion people!

As Americans we still enjoy the greatest privileges in the world today. However, as watchdogs over our freedoms, our liberties, and our pursuit of happiness we need to be aware that, perhaps, we sometimes may give up too much responsibility to places where we need to maintain local control.

Some time ago I was watching a program on The Learning Channel. A Washington University law professor was giving a lecture on the reasons why basic needs in the world aren't being met. The lecture pinpointed the same issue as had the U.S. News and World Report article and emphasized the ability of the world to produce enough food for everyone. So, then we can ask ourselves this question "Why do we have famine in many parts of the world today?" His answer was because of government policy.

The following story is a prime example of what could happen if we let it. For 45 years Haile Selassie ruled Ethiopia under the concept of ***self-determination***. One of the ways he achieved these was that he used education and modern methods of his day to prepare his people for a prosperous society for tomorrow.

Of course, whenever something is tried there is always opposition. Militant forces became a dominant factor in his government and slowly began to suggest reforms. The motivating factor was to eventually take over the Selassie administration. On Sept. 12, 1974, Selassie was overthrown and imprisoned where he shortly died. In time the hardnosed regime began to launch its "reform" by destroying 30,000 people and terrorizing the rest of the population. Surprisingly, and very quickly, his advisors began to establish a new order.

Traditionally Ethiopian farmers had stored food during the good years to prepare themselves for possible bad years, but because of the regime's oppression and usurpation over their rights and liberties the farmers were no longer free to use their food-raising methods of the past; the new government outlawed this practice and called it "hoarding." Peasants had also customarily followed a practice of reinvesting their surplus in their own farms for the sake of expanding production. The new regime denounced this as "capitalist accumulation" and "private investment," which was no longer allowed. Historically, Ethiopian tradesmen who were engaged in food distribution had bought products in the food-surplus areas to sell where there was a shortage of food. The new regime outlawed this practice as "exploitation," and replaced the entire free market system with strictly supervised government commissions (Today we know them as Czars).

The next step was land reform, where peasants were assigned a few acres of land appropriated from large land owners, but these were much too small to justify cultivation with mechanical equipment. Large communes were also established under the government, but these immediately suffered the same crop failures and repeated same the drop-in production that characterized communal farms all over the world.

Within a few years Ethiopia was suffering widespread famine. In less than a decade Ethiopia had gone from being the breadbasket of Africa to one of the poorest and deprived nations of the modern world.[71]

It is a fact that when we lose, or give up, the ability to govern ourselves, other people will do it for us. This is what happened, for instance, with Native Americans when the Bureau of Indian Affairs (BIA) was created and took over trust responsibility of tribes. In reality the BIA was supposed to work itself out of a job when tribes began to

---

[71] At the time I was gathering notes for this writing I never thought we would come even close to this scenario until the first half of the Obama administration was completed. It remains to be seen where the next year takes us if we continue to allow this trend of the federal government interfering with our private lives. The Founding Fathers warned us against this and made the ideas of socialism and communism unconstitutional.

get on their feet and become more and more self-sufficient— however when we look at the history of how the federal government had various policies toward the American Indians from the beginning to now we see, in a nutshell, the issues of assimilation through education during President Jefferson's tenure, to extermination by the policies of the great Indian fighter Andrew Jackson, to reorganization during Roosevelt's term, to self-determination during Carter's time, and a land-mark piece of legislation that started during Reagan's tenure and signed by President Clinton called self-governance. The Public Law 100-422 self-governance demonstration project was a tribally driven initiative that changed dramatically the way the BIA was to work with tribal governments by turning more and more of its programs, services, functions and activities over to capable tribal councils.[72]

As Americans, even in this day and age, we still must fight for our basic rights, so let us not be complacent as to allow anything like what happened to Ethiopia happen to us. We, indeed—I am sure, all want to do the right things. If we are true to that idea then let us do the right things for the right reasons based on right reasoning. Right reasoning, again, is anything that is based upon the Natural Law. When we retain the freedoms to do what we want with our lives, then peace and prosperity will surely follow if we keep ourselves focused on living our lives based on correct principles.

---

[72] *During his campaign candidate Obama came out with a statement about how he was going to benefit Native Americans. In my opinion his statement was weak and didn't mention anything about how he was going to use the self-governance concept to strengthen tribal governments. For the short term, and like everyone else, tribes may benefit from the stimulus packages but for the long term—when the bills are going to become due—it will be upon our children, grandchildren and their children who will be paying these debts. The Founding Fathers said that it was immoral to leave our debts for our grandchildren to pay. It is against the natural order of things.*

THERE OUGHT TO BE A LAW

Thursday, June 6, 2002

Here are some things I've been thinking about for some time. It comes from my understanding, somewhat, about things that are contained in the Declaration of Independence that many people - more so politicians and lawyers, aren't paying too much heed to. It has to do with this equality business and unalienable rights that are supposedly guaranteed to everyone who exists under the banner of the American flag. It also has to do with our natural right to stand up for our natural rights.

It says in the declaration that all men are created equal in the eyes of the Creator. Herein, I believe, is the foundation for all human rights. Now this doesn't mean whether we are black, red, white or yellow that we are created equal economically, socially, or politically. So governments, whether they be national, state, regional or local have no power or authority to try to make us equal in these areas by whatever programs, services, functions or activities they may administer on behalf of the people, for the people, of the people etc.

What I think the Founders meant by this phrase was that we all have the same opportunities to advance ourselves politically, socially and economically if we so wish. Governments whether they be local, regional, state or national are obligated to afford us these rights to their citizens. It is up to us if we want to progress through life as a successful, productive citizen, or if we just want to be a deadbeat. In any event, whatever bed we make for ourselves is our own doing if we are healthy, willing and able to take on the challenges before us.

What about this unalienable right concept? The declaration says that we are endowed by the Creator with certain unalienable rights - that among these are the protection of our lives, our liberties and our pursuit of happiness. It also states that governments were created for that purpose - that is to protect our rights, not take them away. Of course, when we violate our natural right to life, enjoy our liberties, and obtain whatever happiness we are striving for, we eventually suffer the consequences. Then people find reasons for laws to be made. The appeal to the legislatures is that "there ought to be a law." I think the intent of the Founding Fathers was to afford us all the opportunity to do whatever we want with our lives so long as we don't interfere with the right of others to do the same thing. When we begin to interfere with others' rights then laws are made. We come up with this "there ought to be a law" syndrome and now we have so many laws on the books that we can't keep up with enforcing them.

Finally, we can ask ourselves the question: "Do we live in a democracy?" I think we can find the answer quite quickly when we go through the Pledge of Allegiance when it says, "I pledge allegiance to the flag and to the United States of America and to the - what???" Why to the "republic for which we stand." When the Founders debated this to death they thought that it would be dangerous to be a democracy because history has shown that absolute power to the people could lead to anarchy. A republican form of government means that it is a representative of the people and also limited to what it can do. However, to give complete power to a group of people could lead to despotism. So, what they did was make America a republic. It says so in the Constitutions, Article IV, and Section 4. The republican idea allows good people to work for the best interest of the people who put them there. And then it is up to the good people to be the watchdogs. As watchdogs we have an obligation to make sure that these good people do what they are supposed to do and not to become so powerful that governments begin to usurp our rights.

Are we doing our part?

PART FOUR

RECLAIMING OUR HERITAGE

It was the belief of early Native American leaders that—
"Peace might one day be achieved through the power of
the Creator—from sea to shining sea."

Chief White Eyes

RAMIFICATIONS OF FIRST AND SECOND-RATE PEOPLE

January 12, 2003

In a small community folks in charge are under the so-called magnifying glass nearly on a daily basis. In our little town we have gone through some changes in a couple major organizations.

Our village for-profit corporation has undergone a transformation in leadership that has caused major concern among some shareholders. During a shareholder meeting on November 23, 2002 two new board members were elected. This caused a change, also, in the selection of the President and CEO of the corporation. Many shareholders feel that the shift will make no difference because the corporation has been on a downhill trend since the early 1990's. Of course, leadership from the board level will depend on how management will carry forth the goals and objectives, but I understand there is discontent among the board about how the new President will be able to function properly without absolute control over all of the subsidiaries. This has divided the board. The board, over the past many years, has been divided on nearly every issue brought before them. They proclaim that there are a minority and a majority group and because of this division they are unable to move whatever agenda they may have forward. This is a for-profit business, and it should be run like a business—not like a political entity. In my opinion how the leadership brings the issues together for the better remains to be seen. Shareholders are discontent and are presently circulating a recall petition. How far this goes also remains to be seen.

On another issue we have a divided community over the apparent resignation of a popular school principal. Rumor has it that the superintendent and the principal were at odds about a drug and alcohol zero tolerance policy. Two students were allegedly caught smoking pot on the school grounds. In this case the principal was intending to carry out the full condition of the policy whereby the athlete was to sit out a ten-day period from practicing in a sport after the end of the suspension. It was rumored that the superintendent took charge of the incident and waived the ten-day portion of the policy so one student could participate in the sport. The other had to remain suspended.

One issue led to another to a point where the Classified and Unclassified staff in the school held a meeting. A vote was taken and there was an overwhelming support for the principal. Lack of confidence in the superintendent's performance was likewise overwhelming, who was hired in July of 2002.

I always felt that if one were in a hiring and firing position that if he or she was a first-rate person, then he or she would hire first-rate people in his or her company. This holds true with any entity whether it be governmental, a for-profit, non-profit, board or commission organization. Of course, you always want your business or company to be run smoothly and because you do I would think that it would be necessary to follow that charge. If it is a for-profit you'll want to see it generate a profit. A non-profit or governmental entity provides services, and so you want to be certain that the best services are provided for your stakeholders. Outstanding administrators are the key to successes in any well-run organization.

I'm sure we have seen good and bad companies come and go. A business could have a lot of money in the bank, but if bad management is involved, that company is doomed for failure unless management has changed for the better. You know, there is a report out that says that there are about 50,000 new businesses that start up in America every year. The information also says that 50% of those businesses will fail— that 80 % of the reasons why new companies fail is because of imperfect management.

Here is another thought. Richard M. White, Jr., in his book The Entrepreneur's Manual, state's that second-rate people always hire third-rate people. The reason for this scenario is that second-rate people invariably thrive on power and control. Power and control are good only if you delegate it to the proper people, but if one keeps it to themselves, troublesome things happen. I have a friend who is the director of a large organization. He said he loves power. "I love power because I can delegate it to my staff, who will use it wisely."

It's really not that difficult to find able people these days. It is, however, the duty of high-quality leaders to find and hire them.

A NEW KIND OF COMMON SENSE

One day I received an email from a lady whose first name is Nina. I know a Nina or two, but this Nina wasn't anyone I recognized; her email was forwarded from a friend and addressed to a host of other people, of whom most I am also not familiar with. The title of her message was "Sending Old Guys to War"

One notation in her comments was that researchers have drawn a conclusion that 18-year-old boys have their thoughts too much on sex and wouldn't have their psyche set on the tasks at hand. However, she imagines the old guys don't mull over the subject very much. I'm assuming she believes that because older men don't have their mind on the subject as often as the youngsters do, they'd have more time strategizing about how to win a war while the young guys do the fighting. This may be true, but I wonder what these methodical investigators have to say about *dirty old men* in current news every day where there are stories about the abuse of children by older men. Another notion was that young guys haven't lived long enough to be cranky and a cranky soldier is a dangerous warrior. Well—I don't know about this one. Whether you are old or young, when you are in a skirmish and you see your buddies falling all around you, some men will rise to the occasion and do some pretty heroic feats. I recently saw the older version of the movie Alamo. These valiant men lost that battle, but because of their valor—both old and young, the Americans were able to retaliate and subsequently win the war. This is a "man" thing.

Nina's friend further contends that if we can't kill the enemy us old fogies will complain them into submission like: "My back hurts."

Well I'm one of those ole-timers and I have, on more occasions than one, vainly argued this excuse to my wife to swindle myself out of work I've neglected to do for a long time. But I have also gotten into incidences that made pain in my back go away in an instant when it means saving my life—or someone else's. I have experienced some very challenging events in my lifetime—mostly commercial fishing experiences from nearly drifting over the Dry Bay bar in a loaded vessel into foamy breakers to having my skiff float away from me while digging clams on an island at night where the tide came up to my chest before my uncle rescued me—to being pulled overboard by a halibut skate in 40 knot winds and surviving it.

My daughter has been keeping track. She contends that I am like a cat and have nine lives. One day she observed, "Dad, you've used six of them up. You've got three more left." From these experiences I have learned a lot about how that adrenaline can make us, both young and old, do some amazing things.

Another complaint she says we ole-timers may have is, "I'm hungry."

Sounds more like what a youngster would say. As an old timer, I really don't require much food—not as much as I did when I was a thriving teenager anyway; in those days I was always famished.

It's a natural thing.

It's a boy thing.

Now that we have kicked our children out of the house—and now that they are on their own and raising their own families, our grandchildren are the ones who have those ravenous appetites. My wife is constantly preparing food and making goodies for them—usually there isn't much left over and so she tries to make me serve as the garbage disposer.

"How come you're not eating this food?" she'd say. "It's just going to waste."

Well, simply put, I'm not interested. I really don't need that much food these days, although I will never turn down a meal at a potlatch or community gathering. Despite that fact, I am always reminded about my mother's famous comment when we kids stuck our nose up at food we didn't like: "You know, there are a lot of children around the world who are starving." Sometimes that guilt trick worked, other times it didn't.

Or another good one is: "Where's the remote control?"

Now, I can identify with that one. Being a couch potato is right down my alley, but I'll tell you, if I were to live my life over and the likes of Osama Ben Laden were around in my prime of life, I would have gladly left my father home to risk my well-being to give him the opportunity, and others, the chance to live to be a ripe old age.

Sadly, he didn't but, like many others from his generation, he deserved it.

GOVERNMENT FOR THE IRAQIS, OF THE IRAQIS, BY THE IRAQIS

Monday, April 21, 2003

Now that the war in Iraq is winding down[73] and there is diverse discussion about mostly war activities to bring civil government to these people, the United Nations now thinks it can play a part in promoting democracy and self-government to the liberated people of Iraq. Now no one has admitted that this will be an easy task and I'm not saying that it will be a piece of cake either. But what we need to be focused on is the goal of helping the Iraqis people to be governed by the Iraqis, for the Iraqis and of the Iraqis.

Now after seeing all that had transpired and what I have learned over the past three or four weeks, I keep asking myself whether those countries that have the deciding votes in the UN will make this happen.

We have seen how France, Russia and Germany voted on the resolution to use force only a month ago. It was mainly the United States and Britain who were stalwarts in seeing this war through from beginning to end. I was puzzled at why Russia, Germany, and France were just as stalwart against the war on the onset. And then about midway through all the conflict, I was troubled by the discovery about how each of these countries had an indirect part in the war. Russian tanks and weapons were used by the Iraqis troops; they trained the

---

[73] As of this date the war is still going on.

Iraqis how to use these weapons. France also contributed weapons and ammunition. And then the Germans—they were the one who were contracted to design and build those bunkers under those elaborate palaces of Saddam Hussein. Sure—someone will argue that the United States helped Iraqi years ago with training and weapons, but we never hide that fact.

Now hear this—. We all know the United Nations is comprised of members of a host of countries and since its early stages; the majority of General Secretaries have been from socialistic or communist countries. Even though the purpose of the UN is to promote and foster peace throughout the world, if you monitor those who had the capacity to manipulate you'll find that reluctance to accomplish its mission was forestalled in many ways. Look at the Somalia and Bosnia aftermaths. The UN's attempts to bring civil government into these countries in actual fact never happened.

Many people in early days of the UN felt that the Unites States should have no part of it and that we would be more effective by means of dealing with countries on an individual basis through our ambassadors. Yep—I think our ambassadors will do a better job dealing with troubled countries than the so-called policies of the U.N. Here is why.

We are experts at developing credentials that foster freedom, liberty and the pursuit of happiness. Look at our own history and what we accomplished. Falling short of a miracle the Founding Fathers were visionaries. Doesn't the Good Book say somewhere that "Where there is no vision, people parish"? The vision must be virtuous, however. Contrast that with the so-called illusions of Saddam, Hitler, Stalin, Castro and other dictators. Even though I may have some thoughts about where our governments are out of compliance at this day and age, we still have the expertise, knowledge and the were-with-all to assist broken countries struggling for freedom and democracy.

And then there are factions of experts who believe that the diverse people in Iraq will never agree to any one form of government. It is true as true can be, but review, if you will, the diverse people who constructed the principles we cherish. Of course, I believe that people have the right to disagree with the way our governments are functioning, but men of vision fostered this as a hallowed birthright. Hopefully, when Iraq is settled they may still have the privilege of doing so, but in an organized manner rather than the anarchy we have witnessed since Baghdad was over-run by the coalition troops.

Well back to the UN's involvement. We can let it play a part—perhaps on a limited bases like performing the humanitarian responsibility. Perhaps then, they will learn a little about human nature.

What I don't see happening right now in Iraq is that there doesn't seem to be a George Washington emerging from the ranks of the Iraqi people. I believe it will take someone like that to excite the Iraqi population to winning this war for the sake of freedom and liberty.

THE SPIRIT IN SIT

Sunday, July 14, 2002

Many, many years ago, when I began to get some notoriety as a writer, I asked Harvey Milton, a Tlingit elder, if he knew any stories about glaciers and their relationship with our people. His reply was that he wasn't going to tell me anything because I would write about it and get rich. I never pursued the issue after that.

When the Hubbard Glacier blocked Russell Fiord in May of 1986 the event attracted worldwide attention. Major media networks came to Yakutat to observe and report on the phenomenon; even people from Save the Whales coalition were concerned about animals that were trapped in the fjord. As liquefied ice doused off the surrounding glaciers it raised the fjord 12 to 18 inches a day. People feared it would eventually spill over the southern end of the fjord and flood into the Situk River, a world-class steelhead-producing river and mainstay for the local people for commercial, sport and subsistence purposes. This, indeed, would have altered the make-up of the Situk River system and transformed it from a fresh-water-lake-fed river into a glacier river.

I remember attending a public meeting set up by the media with a group of elders; they were interested in learning how the Natives related to the glacier. No one at that time shared any information. I'm not sure if they didn't know or if they weren't willing to share what they thought might be sacred stories, or whether they knew anything at all.

Kadashan Speaks: The Law of Nature and Nature's God

A couple of days later Harvey invited me to his home. "If anyone is going to get rich from this story, then I am going to tell you. It might as well be you," he said.

"A long time ago, maybe a thousand years ago, the glacier extended from Point Manby across to Ocean Cape. That's why you see those shallow shoals that goes across the bay, that's where the glacier ended.

"One time some Copper River people were crossing the glacier to trade with the Yakutat Tlingits. They brought the copper with them to trade. One of their dogs fell into a deep crevice. It never came back. The people, they continued with their journey and made it across the glacier to Monti Bay. They named it Yaakwdaat, which means in their language a 'peaceful lagoon to park your canoes.'

"Very soon after that the glacier began to move back real fast. It took maybe three, four hundred years to get to where it is now—thirty miles from the mouth of Yakutat Bay into where it is restlessly snuggled next to the mountains. Now it moves back and forth pretty fast. It always was that way since the dog fell into the crack of the glacier.

"It's the spirit in sit (glacier) that is causing it to move like that. It's restless, and the glacier will move like that until we have a potlatch for the spirit of that dog to send it to the spirit world of the Tlingits."

In October 1986 the dam broke and the glacier retreated. The trapped animals saved themselves and everything eventually returned back to normal. However, the glacier continued to retreat and advance and it still does today. Scientists predict it eventually would close again and when it does it would be permanent. If the closing will be a permanent like they think, it will take about two to three months for the fjord to raise enough to begin spilling into Situk and Mountain Lakes and turn the Situk River into a glacier river. Scientists have theorized that perhaps when the river begins to restore itself that it might improve to be even better than it is now. This may take up to five years or longer, however. As tribal President of the Yakutat Tlingit Tribe, and as a member of the Southeast Regional Subsistence Regional Advisory Council, I have the opportunity to talk to many people. I asked one biologist what he thought about the river becoming a glacier river and how would that affect the salmon runs. His reply was that salmon like water. The fact that the Russell Fjord will provide thirty miles of new habitat may change the world for the better. History has told us that this same thing happened about two hundred years ago, and the new flooding turned the Situk River into what it is today—the most productive Salmon River in the world.

It will take time to restore. If it takes that long the sports fishers can always go somewhere else to satisfy their quest for jocular adventure but the people of Yakutat, who depend on the resources from the Situk River system will, indeed, have to investigate other places to obtain their subsistence resources and earn their living from other means until the restoration and enhancement takes place.

Perhaps we need to look at this from a realistic sense and figure out a way in which to send that dog's spirit into the spirit world. I'm not sure, but it's something to think about.

THINGS DON'T HAPPEN BY CHANCE

When I was in college I took this Indian Education course. Our instructor was a Native American and he gave this imposing lecture about the Natural Law. He alleged that long before the foreigners came to the Americas our people lived with nature. Because we lived with nature we understood the laws of nature; because we understood the laws of nature we obeyed the natural laws; and because we obeyed these laws the natural world provided us with all we needed to sustain our lives. When the pilgrims came to our shores, Native Americans helped them survive their winter, teaching them how to live within that circle of nature. For 200 years these people lived in harmony with one another, and with nature. Each year we celebrate Thanksgiving for this purpose.

Our instructor explained that there were outside forces that eventually came to upset that balance. These people were on the outside looking in; their purpose was to enter in and conquer. When they eventually did they caused this turmoil, this culture clash that we are still struggling to overcome today. Now, I believe, this instability has spilled into our entire society.

At the end of his lecture our professor said, "Now it may take some of you a lifetime - others of you will discover this sooner - but when you have learned how we can live within that circle of the Natural Laws, then you have an obligation to share it with the world."

Now over the many years I have read from the best books (including the Good Book), deliberated the philosophies of men, pondered in my heart about correct principles, and appealed to the Creator for a sufficient amount of insight to share what I discovered about the Law of Nature. I do know this: there are principles of life that we must all learn to abide by if we want to enjoy the benefits the Creator has to offer us.

There's this book I read many years ago called *The Chance World*. The author created a world where everything happened by chance. For example, he showed how, if a person jumped from a cliff, there was a good chance that he might fall up instead of down. He also explained how, if a farmer planted asparagus there was a good chance, when harvest time came, that it might sprout peas or some other thing. He used many other examples as well, but when I finished the book I realized something of great significance: We do not live in a chance world. We, indeed, live in a universe of law and order.

And so, I think we should aspire to better understand these laws so that we can use them for our benefit. For instance, we know that water freezes at 32 degrees Fahrenheit. We also know at what temperature it boils. We may never know how the water knows when it reaches these temperatures, but it never makes a mistake. My wife and I use this law to our individual advantage every day. I call it the Battle of the Thermostat. My first duty when I get out of bed each day is to adjust the thermostat to a comfortable level. A couple of hours later my wife is up. She adjusts the temperature a few degrees higher. In a while I am sweltering, so I turn it down. When she begins to get uncomfortable, she turns it back up. This goes on all day.

Consider, if you will, the planets in the universe. They have their own orbits around the sun; they travel at various speeds, and they never bump into one another. It has always been amazing to me how these orders of events function the way they do until I began to do all this researching, studying and pondering in my heart about these things.

Nope! I'm convinced things don't happen by chance. I think this very wise Indian Education professor was challenging us to discover, for ourselves, those principles of truth that apply to everyone, whether we are rich or poor, white or black or otherwise. And when we make any significant discoveries, then we must share them because as I said before" truth does, indeed, belong to everyone."

A BORN-AGAIN WHAT?

Sunday, November 10, 2002

You have heard the phrase, "I am a born-again Christian." While I might embrace a faith that gives me a blueprint for life, I think the most important time for me was when I took an interest in who I really was.

My grandmother instilled a sense of Indianness in me when she began to teach her grandchildren the Tlingit language, songs and dances at an early age. I can scarcely remember how whenever she knew my brother and I approached her doorstep she would begin to sing and tap her cane on the floor. Immediately we would start to dance through the threshold of her door to her chant.

My parents couldn't do this for us because they came from that generation of youngsters who were educated in boarding schools. They were forbidden to speak or practice their ancestral customs because the federal government and the Christian church's goals were to assimilate the Natives into the American society. When they married, and began to raise families, they were mentally incapable to reinforce our history, culture or language into us. While I have friends who speak the language fluently, this is attributed to what happened in their homes, and what never happened in mine.

When I was 7, my father moved the family from Yakutat to Juneau where he secured a job with a construction company. We were taken from the influence of our grandmother. That special connection we enjoyed with her was never renewed, and, much to my regret, I, to this day, feel somewhat displaced because I am unable to even rudimently speak my ancestral language.[74]

I have, however, for the past 25 or so years, taken a concentrated interest in learning about the history and culture of my people. Not only that of my own heritage, but of American history in general.

When I began to understand more about our people's code of behavior, I began to grow with appreciation, realizing also that they had a complex protocol in everything they did.

Let's take, for instance, a brief account from a young man's life. When he was 7 or 8 years old it was his uncle's responsibility to educate (discipline) the youngster. When he reached the age of an adolescent he was trained to hunt, fish and survive, and he was also taught his history and practiced his traditions and culture. When he grew older he traveled among other tribes, sometimes for many years to other Tlingits, Tsimshian's or Haida's in their region, or it could be to the Aleuts along the Aleutians or the Athabascans from the Interior. We do know, also, that the Tlingits traveled as far south as California to trade. It was through these experiences he learned other people's history, songs, dances, etc. Then he returned home to be of service to his people. It was the same as sending our young people away to college in these days and time.

Take, for instance, my great grandfather, Kadashan, of whom I was named after, and who was raised in this manner. He was trained in these same protocols, and when he became a young man he, Toyotta and Sitka Charlie used their knowledge to guide the world traveler, John Muir, through the inside passage of the southeast Alaska panhandle. When he took Muir into Glacier Bay, the Muir Glacier was named after him, but we know who took him there. There is a bay on Chichagof Island across from Tenakee Springs named after the Kadashan family called Kadashan Bay, and there was a "jeep" aircraft carrier built during the Second World War that was christened the Kadashan Bay.

---

[74] Since this article appeared in the Empire, for the past two years I have been taking a course in the Tlingit language. I am learning very slowly, but proud of the fact that I am sticking with it.

Kadashan Speaks: The Law of Nature and Nature's God

Native Americans were deep-rooted in their spiritual beliefs, too. They knew and understood their Creator. To survive in their environments, they had to have a strong belief in a higher being. Their reliance and very survival are reflected upon their belief in the Creator. In fact, like all other religions throughout the world, the God we knew is, and was, the same God the missionaries tried to convert us to. Education was an important part of our society.

Native American history and culture, like other so-called civilized cultures, was transferred from one generation to the other. Today we have been introduced to another way of learning, of which our history and culture is no longer a part. Nowadays we embrace a religion that recognizes the same Creator as Christianity, yet we were forbidden to practice worshipping in our way.

So, in a sense, we can say that we are, too, born-again Christians. As for me, even though I admit to embracing that faith, when I began to learn more about my history along with who I really was —when I found out that I was named after my great-grandfather, Kadashan, and what he did—my chest began to fill with pride, my confidence and self-esteem were bolstered to new heights.

I have heard from our elders many a time that when our language goes, then goes our culture. My wife is a fluent speaker of our language. She grew up with it and has not only learned the language so that our tribal government has her teaching it, but she also learned the history and culture of our Tlingit heritage in the Yakutat area. The past year I have been taking classes in the Tlingit language and am, indeed, struggling with grasping it. I have a three-year-old granddaughter who is taking the language classes too and she is learning the words a lot fast than I am. Now I regret the fact that I have missed out on a lot of who I am, and who my people were. However, from what I am learning, I now find a sense of identity as I learn this difficult language and am becoming a better person because of it.

Indeed, I am becoming a born-again Indian, not so much as I'd like, but it's a beginning.

IS GOD ON OUR SIDE ANYMORE?

Monday, May 10, 2004

Two things impressed me about the men of the USS Kadashan Bay: their patriotism and belief in God.

Last fall I attended, for the first time, a Kadashan Bay Reunion in Reno, Nevada. This gathering included nearly two hundred survivors from a World War II aircraft carrier named after Kadashan Bay located on the northern part of Chichagof Island near Tenakee Springs in Southeast Alaska. For two days I mingled with about two hundred of these remarkable veterans. The youngest is seventy-seven years fresh and the eldest is ninety-nine. The USS Sitkoah Bay and USS Kassan Bay were two other such carriers christened after bays in Southeast Alaska. These escort carriers were called "Jeep Carriers" because they were much smaller than the regular ones; their purpose was to escort the larger carriers and supply them with aircraft missing in combat. I was amazed at the fact that of the thousand men that were on board the ship, there are about 400 left.

They began having their reunions in 1993.

I learned about them in 1997.

Since then I have communicated with a small number of these men and have been invited to attend their reunions and was able to finally do so last October.

At the beginning of their meetings they always had their Chaplin open with a prayer, and then all arose to pledge allegiance to the flag. I asked a bunch of them how they felt about that phrase "one nation under God" in the Pledge of Allegiance. Every one of them believed that it should stay. I asked them "Why?" They all had their answers but the best one I heard was "Because God is on our side."

And so, I am appalled that we have people living under the banner of the American flag who actually believe the phrase is offensive because they may not believe in a Supreme Being. Remember about a year ago I made the point that every nation has a religion they cuddle? America embraced the principles of Christianity—it is evident in every part of our fleeting history. Remember, also, that one of the reasons why the colonist left their homeland was because they were forbidden the freedom to worship the Creator according to the dictates of their conscience. Ole King George—he dissolved the Catholic Church and created the Church of England. No one could go to any other church but this one.

Well, we know, when the Funders framed the Bill of Rights they penned in Amendment I that "Congress shall make no law respecting an establishment of religion, or prohibiting the exercise thereof—" What the Founders meant by this was that our government would be restricted from doing what King George did—that is establish a religion that we all had to abide by. It also says in the same sentence that we would not be forbidden to worship whomever or whatever we had a fancy to. This is the freedom of religion we always hear about. Some people like to utter the fact that this separates the two institutions of church and state; it does—to a degree. Religion, in their opinion, should not play a role in government; however, our Founders recognized that our faith does, indeed, play an important part in our lives. And, like it or not, America was founded upon faith in the Creator—the Christian one.

Review our history; observe what we have been able to accomplish in a short period of time. I am convinced America could not have accomplished what it has without the sponsorship of Devine Providence.

After my experiences in this reunion, I think about these valiant men often—especially now, when we are facing so much adversity; this is a time when we certainly need to exercise our faith. I wonder what will happen to America when the likes of these "defenders of the faith" are gone.

It won't be long.

The Saddam Hussein's and Osama Bin Laden's, and other tyrants, will never triumph over America from without. If we are not watchful, we will go the way of other great nations that have come and gone: through erosion from within.

Eliminating God from the Allegiance is just another step in that direction.

SOCIALISM

What with private industries going to the federal government and begging for bail-outs of billions of dollars to save their companies for the sake of saving jobs, the word socialism has emerged as a conversation piece lately. In one of my recent articles I made this comment:

"Another issue that the Founders warned future generations about was that government should not be in the business of competing with private enterprises. They understood that businesses, particularly small businesses, would drive the economy of this nation. Therefore, for the central government to interfere with this kind of prosperity would eventually lead to socialism."

This was the only time that I mentioned socialism in any of my writings—so far, but it should be now a matter of conversation around the dinner table, during coffee breaks and in public meetings whenever possible. What I am going to do here is talk about socialism to educate people about this precarious theory. And then it will be up to you to decide what direction this great nation is going.

Many celebrated thinkers throughout history have warned the world about the dangers of implementing socialistic ideas, and what would happen if we give in to it. There are various forms of socialism and I will mention those that I studied when I was taking this course in the U.S. Constitution while at Brigham Young University. The founder of the institute who developed this course of study was W. Cleon Skousen. Mr. Skousen used to work for the Federal Bureau of Investigation during J.

Edgar Hoover's tenure as FBI czar. He also wrote several books — but a couple of the most notable were **The Naked Communist, The Making of America** and **The 5000 year Leap**. He also wrote a series of articles called *The Works of W. Cleon Skousen* of which most of the research for this writing is referenced; I have also used thoughts from the writings of Frederick Bastiat from his treatise called **The Law**.

Skousen says that, *"The ultimate goal of all forms of socialism is to have government ownership of all means of production."* He identifies essentially five forms of socialism. It would be well if everyone understood these, so we can recognize them when they start illuminating through casual, serious conversation or, even deliberately, emerging in our governmental systems.

Communism is an interesting concept. Its purpose is to spread socialism on an international scale by using terrorism tactics, violence and subversion by means of propaganda aimed at other nations as if it were at war with a country. Leaders could be at a table with other nations and at the same time preparing for deliberate, aggressive war against one of the nations they are negotiating with.

Nazism is an abbreviated word for National Socialism. Hitler used this tactic by means of his military force to conquer one country at a time. His purpose was to set up a socialistic dictatorship in those countries his armies invaded and then eventually control all of Europe— and the world. He nearly succeeded!

Fascism is another form of National Socialism—it was instigated in Italy by Mr. Benito Mussolini during the Second World War, but it was very short lived.

Fabian Socialism is a deceptive type of socialism. The idea here is for the government to take control over people's lives and property while explaining a fantastic idea as they convincingly illustrate how a new, unproved program will help the unfortunate.

Democratic Socialism is a system of promoting socialism by achieving its objective to take control of production by peaceful means and by getting the people's consent to do so. The people who promoted this type of socialism learned that they could only achieve this by appealing to individual economic groups like—, for instance, the farmer is convinced that practicing a little bit of socialism will take the risk out of farming, or the industrial worker is told that most of their profits will go to the worker, or that the businessman is duped into the idea that socialism will arrange the economy so that competition is limited—and people with these ideas appeal to the government to make this all happen.

All these ideas, especially when we are in a crisis or emergency, are used as an excuse to greatly increase taxes. The proponents of socialism will constantly look to the government to solve problems that affect the poor, the sick, the unemployed, the elderly, the young, the bankrupt and on and on and on——and the idea is to take from the have's and give to the half not's or, as the term most recently used, to "redistribute wealth."

Following is the opening statement in the introduction of Frederic Bastiat's treatise **The Law:**

Frederic Bastiat (1801-1850) was a French economist, statesman, and author. He did most of his writing during the years just before - and immediately following —the Revolution of February 1848. This was the period when France was rapidly turning to complete socialism. As a Deputy to the Legislative Assembly, Mr. Bastiat was studying and explaining each socialist fallacy as it appeared. And he explained how socialism must inevitably degenerate into communism. But most of his countrymen chose to ignore his logic.

The Law is here presented again because the same situation exists in America today as in the France of 1848. The same socialist-communist ideas and plans that were then adopted in France are now sweeping America. The explanations and arguments then advanced against socialism by Mr. Bastiat are —word for word —equally valid today. His ideas deserve a serious hearing.

And indeed, this is true to this day and age.

The Founding Fathers recognized the principles of socialism as a deadly threat to our unalienable right to life, liberty, property and pursuit of happiness. Here is a statement made by one of the foremost Founders, Samuel Adams: "***The utopian* schemes of leveling (re-distribution** of wealth) and a community of goods (central ownership of all the means of production and distribution), are as visionary and impracticable as those which vest all property in the crown." He went on to say that these ideas "are arbitrary, despotic, and in this government they just created was unconstitutional."

Thomas Jefferson warned future generations and anticipated the day when the government would seek to excuse heavy taxation on the basis that it was necessary to help the poor. He said, *"If we can prevent the government from wasting the labors of the people, under the pretense of taking care of them, they must be happy."*

When the Founders gathered themselves in Constitutional Hall in Philadelphia they painstakingly drafted in our Constitution a formula for success. They also warned that when people begin picking away at the Constitution for the sake of helping the poor and unfortunate, then they use the excuse that the idea is justified. In W. Cleon Skousen's closing paragraphs in his book **The Making of America,** *The Substance and the Meaning of the Constitution* he pens this:

It is helpful to remember that the Constitution is not a stale, dead document. Rather, it is a vital, living blueprint for the success of the United States as a nation and its citizens as individuals.

He also adds this in the following paragraph: A quick comparison between the constitutional principles and our practices today will show where we have gone astray. And the remedy is simple: return to the basic principles of the Founders' formula.

His final paragraph says this as a challenge to us all: The first step to improvement and reform is education. The next step is action. The principles of the Constitution were not meant only to be studied but to be applied.

That then, is our challenge today.

THE IMPACT OF SOCIALISM IN THE UNITED STATES

June 22, 2009

In a previous article I talked about how I became a political isolationist. When I was dissatisfied with the way our politicians were running the country, I stepped back and looked at what party advocated the values I embraced. As a young man I was very liberal during my first two years of college. But when I came home to my village after Kennedy was assassinated and Lyndon Johnson's Great Society[75] took hold and saw how it affected the small community of Yakutat Alaska, I changed my views and became a conservative scholar. As a result, I changed my political affiliation. I also learned a lot in college about the political spectrum and how the Founding Fathers preferred the government to operate from the middle of that spectrum— that it was up to the voters to keep the political machine in balance to align with what is called *people's law (see chart below)*. Not so today folks. Let me explain by referring to some of my notes from the Constitutional Seminar I took while at Brigham Young University

    First—as in all other parts of the world through its recorded history socialism had been tried and it never, never, never worked![76] After the turn of the 20th century there was a group of wealthy Americans who

---

[75] See The Constitutional Eagle in the Archives.
[76] See article SOCIALISM where it explains the five types of socialism.

began to advocate the concepts of democratic socialism.⁷⁷ These were prominent and respected Americans:

1. Andrew Carnie was one of the giants in the steel industry
2. J.P. Morgan was one of America's foremost railroad magnets
3. John D. Rockefeller was one of America's chief oil giants.

There were others, but I believe these guys were *wolves in sheep clothing, who* turned away from the Constitution and began embracing the principles of democratic socialism. Why do you suppose democratic socialism appealed to them? Because democratic socialism provides a concentration of power over people and their property and it offered some advantages to international bankers operating in the United States as well as over multi-national corporations by:

1. <u>Gradually</u> acquiring leadership of both political parties. If they could accomplish this they would gain control of the policies of the government.⁷⁸
2. The power of government could then be used to <u>gradually</u> establish cartel privileges which would diminish this problem of competition of which they were sorely afraid of.
3. These men's goal (were capitalists in the beginning) was to acquire control over the nation's money and credit system.
4. The government would then be able to increase taxes and expand government spending that would enrich their own enterprises. You see, these charlatans used capitalism to prosper so they could use their wealth to gain more control over the affairs of government and to eventually advocate expansion of government for their own benefit. These elaborate programs were used to socialize the American system to:
    a. Channel hundreds of millions of dollars through tax-exempt foundations to provide grants to educational

---

⁷⁷ See article on Socialism for definition of democratic socialism
⁷⁸ See Constitutional Eagle graph below.

systems. Eventually the government would take control of education by sinking money into the system. (He who pulls the purse strings always has the final say). Socialistic ideas will have been taught in the college and universities and we would gradually have a society focused on bringing America to its knees by taking away our freedoms and liberties.

b. All of these heavily financed programs emphasized a collectivist or socialistic system as the hope of the future. Also, they would convince people that the ideas of the Founding Fathers were obsolete because they did not fit in with the economic styles of the time.

c. They also believed that the Constitution was obsolete.

d. So then, these wealthy leaders would invest a lot of money and resources in certain political candidates who would promote socialistic ideas after they were elected into office.[79]

e. They began to buy up many important channels of the media (newspapers, radio, TV.) to promote socialistic ideas.

f. Their most loyal employees were pressed forward to accept top-level government offices where policies and decisions were to be made.[80] In 1913, behind the scenes of course, they <u>eventually</u> had a lot of influences in the Whitehouse and Congress. It was in this year when three important programs were pushed through.

The Federal Reserve System was created, which gave a consortium of wealthy bankers control over the money and credit system of the United States; the Sixteenth Amendment[81] to the Constitution went into effect, which gave the Federal government a powerful financial resource: taxing on our incomes. The other was the 17th Amendment

---

[79] Look at Obama's Czars
[80] Abide
[81] See The Power To Tax The Power to Destroy

which made Senators elected by the people instead of appointed by the State Legislatures. The result of this amendment caused States Rights to be critically violated and state influence would eventually erode.

This is outrageous, because since then (and we've seen it more in this administration than any other) every emergency has been used as an excuse to increase taxes, take over private enterprises, strengthen federal regulation through stimulus packages and <u>gradually</u> focus the whole power of government away from the individual, and local self-government, toward Washington.

Well—even though the Carnegie's, the Morgan's, and Rockefeller's may have started the socialistic (progressive) movement at the turn of the 20th century Americans who believed in **_people's law_** managed to prevail and keep the principles embedded in the Constitution intact. Weak attempts have been made to socialize America, but **_people's law_** kept it at arm's length for as long as possible.

Now we have a young, brilliant, man who was graduated with a constitutional law degree from Harvard, trained by the likes of Bill Ayers on socialistic ideas as a young man, was counseled for twenty years by the Reverend Wright (who wants God to <u>damn</u> America) and trained by Acorn about how to a organize a socialistic community. The progressive movement has moved out of the closet and is now interring into our lives.

Wake up America!

RECONCILIATION—IS IT CONSTITUTIONAL?

Thursday, March 10, 2009

It looked like when the health bill the democrats had tried to shove on the American people, before the election of Scott Brown, had become a dead issue— for the time being at least. Well not so, because the President has submitted his own version, which I understand is not much different than the Senate bill—and will cost more. On February 25th, there was a health summit, which the President and the democrats were unable to agree with the republicans, and now it looks like, according to Harry Reed, an attempt to jam this thing down our throats will be tried again. The question we need to ask ourselves, then, is reconciliation Constitutional?

Mr. Reed said that reconciliation has been used since 1981. So, was there an amendment to the Constitution that authorized this?

We should all know by now that Congress, or the President, cannot do anything that the Constitution does not authorize. I think I mentioned in another article what the Constitution formed a government that had checks and balances built into it. I also talked about the constitutional eagle and how it keeps balance in our governments. Essentially it is this: The Constitution was designed to keep the government in check and the government's purpose is to keep you and me from getting into mischief.

In the government there are the three branches—the legislative, judicial and the executive arms. The Founders designed it this way so that the government could never over extend itself above the people. We have learned in school that the legislative branch's purpose is to make the laws, the judicial interprets the laws, and the executive branch carries the laws out. For some time now, we have seen presidents make laws through his executive orders, and the courts through its interpretations.

In the essay I wrote a year ago called The Constitutional Eagle, I had a graph drawn at the end of the article in my website: www.kadashan.simplesitecom. It showed how both the republicans and democrats had moved way over to the left side of the spectrum. This is very dangerous because it does not have any way to check or provide balance in the way government is supposed to function.

It used to be that we could distinguish the difference between a democrat and a republican. Well not so today. In another of my essays I mentioned that there is no difference—and there really isn't. Here is why:

We no longer have a conservative bunch anymore, nor a liberal group that are <u>true</u> to their ideals. The political parties have been transforming—and transforming for a long time. We've identified with liberals or conservatives in the past, but today we hear a lot about people on the left and people on the right. What it has really boiled down to these days is conservatism and progressives.

The progressive ideas started filtering into our governmental systems around the first of the last century—starting with President Woodrow Wilson and escalated through Franklin D. Roosevelt's presidency. It may have been thwarted somewhat after that but then the movement went underground. But it has been progressively filtering into our governmental system ever since. Now they are pretty much out of the wood work. Hillary Clinton admitted she was a democratic progressive. President Obama's special advisors, known as Crazes, are progressives who emerged from the radical 60's and 70's. Here is what is so frightening about progressives:

Progressives have no regard or respect for the Constitution. Their purpose is to have the government take over all means of production by interfering with businesses, banks, health care and a host of other things that will make it impossible for the average American to succeed in a free market society. In a nutshell progressives believe that governments should manage the economy.

The thing that is so obvious about this is that in the progressive movement there are both democrat and republicans. Since the last Presidential election progressives have shifted the balance of power on the political spectrum to the far left. No longer balance here anymore. It's all one sided and slanting more and more to socialism.

When the President took his oath of office he pledged to support the Constitution and laws of the United States. What he was pledging was to govern from the middle. Many presidents have gone astray at times, attempting to take the country either far too right or left of the spectrum. The American people have always brought them back to reality. President Clinton tried this with his own health care package—he had to retreat and start governing more toward the middle when he got chastised by the American people in 1994.

Not so with this president. Even though he has suffered a couple of setbacks he, along with Pelosi and Reed, have been determined to jam his health care through Congress at the expense of their party and endangering a lot of democrats getting back into the respective offices in the next election.

I love what Thomas Jefferson said about political extremists. He was referring to the Federalists of his day as a homogeneous body. He said that:

> *"Under that name lurks the heretical sect of monarchists (today's progressives). These men have no right to office—anywhere, and if it be known to the President, the oath he has taken to support the Constitution imperiously requires the instantaneous*

dismission of such officer; and I hold the President criminal if he permitted such to remain."

Thus, we know why the Founders wanted presidents to govern from the middle. A democrat, as an example, may govern slightly left, and a republican slightly right—but to the extreme on either side is dangerous to our wellbeing—and our health. With this information I am not ashamed to declare our President a criminal. H should be impeached, but no one in congress is brave enough to start the process. Just talk, but no action.

Now back to reconciliation—is it constitutional or not? I think not, because with such a large piece of legislation before Congress, which involves every American alive today and into the future, would require a constitutional amendment. It requires two thirds vote of both the House and Senate and two thirds of the states—much too long to get done. So nearly thirty years ago they invented reconciliation as a rule in the Senate to address emergency situations. Well—what about the Constitution's mandate that "no law should be made without the consent of the governed?"

We may deserve a right to health care, but the American people should have a say about how it should be administered to us. The Commerce Clause is a bad excuse for passing the Obama Care program. Health care is a product, and Americans should be able to purchase it from the free market.

And it should be constitutional.

A POLITICAL ISOLATIONIST

May 19, 2009

In a previous article I shared how I embraced the republican platform on the political spectrum called the Constitutional Eagle.[82] I also said that I would often step back and look at where we are and may take a stand as a political isolationist because I may be unhappy with where any party may be leading us.

As you can see when the wings of the eagle are spread out there is this horizontal scale that tells us where we can fit into the scheme of the body politic. When I was attending Brigham Young I had this history instructor, William Fox, who developed a syllabus for our course of study; I still have it today and review it every now and then; one of his lectures dealt with this horizontal/vertical approach to our political engines. He stressed that the Founders believed that if we kept this horizontal concept in sight that this would keep America balanced as a nation because the voters would tend to keep the government operating from the middle, which would align closer to what is known as ***people' law***. However, he warned that there may come a time in our lives when an attempt would be made to try the vertical approach and said that this was not good.

Now I have always been amazed at how the Americans have been pretty good at keeping the politicians on the horizontal spectrum the past 75 or more years, however there were strong attempts to strategize

---

[82] See The Spectrum of the Constitutional Eagle

ways in which to translate the political range from horizontal to vertical, but the common-sense Americans were able to combat any threats of this. There is a great danger when we allow the spectrum to become vertical. The danger is that if we let the vertical line go to the extreme right it would eventually lead to tyranny. On the other hand, when the vertical line swings extremely to the left we have too much government control which leads us toward anarchy.[83] When there are no government people will run wild—when there is too much then people begin to lose their freedoms and liberties.

The Founders believed in the two-party systems because the purpose was to keep the body politics balanced. However, the danger of swinging left or right is risky when both parties swing to one side at the same time. That is what has been happening within the last few months since Obama was sworn in as our President. We are, indeed, treading down the road to socialism.

Socialism has been a threat to our freedoms for a long time, but never so strong and evident as with this administration. It appeared like some liberal congressmen were waiting for the likes of Nancy Pelosi and Harry Reed to come on the scene— and then just waiting for a time when they can implement liberal policies in the guise of trying to nationalize health care, take from the have's and give to the have-nots, fix social security, run businesses and well— you name it.

The thing that really triggered all this was spearheaded by the former administration, a president who dubbed himself a compassionate conservative. I often wondered what a compassionate conservative was, so as I watched him try to take care of the <u>wants</u>, rather than the <u>needs,</u> of the American people his budget got bigger and bigger—this is contrary to the conservative philosophy of limited government. Here is when the danger sets in because the Republican Party slid over to the left with the democrats. The democrats have always been there, but when President Bush's stimulus package passed, it made it easier for the new administration to further the cause by taking over the insurance business, banks and the auto industry. I was very disappointed when

---

[83] See the chart at the end of the article The Impacts of Socialism

John McCain supported and voted for Bush's so-called stimulus package. When Bush invited him and Obama to Washington in the middle of their campaigns to get their support I knew that Obama would have no problem supporting it, but I expected McCain to stick to the republican core values and oppose it— oppose it vigorously. Instead I was vigorously disappointed.

I was disappointed because I know that the Constitution guarantees us a republican form of government. This concept is based on a limited central government which means that the central government should be small in nature.

I also gave a pretty good definition of socialism in another article under that name and quoted W. Cleon Skousen's statement that "— t**he ultimate goal of all forms of socialism is to have government ownership of all means of production."** That's exactly what our central government is trying to do now—as we speak. The article also mentions five types of socialism: communism, Nazism, Fabian socialism, fascism, and democratic socialism. *Democratic Socialism* is a system of promoting socialism by achieving its objective to take control of production by peaceful means and by getting the people's consent to do so. The charisma of our present president is mesmerizing the American people so that they will agree to anything he says. Be aware of "wolves in sheep's clothing."

The people who promoted this type of socialism learned that they could only achieve this by appealing to individual economic groups— like the farmer is convinced that practicing a little bit of socialism will take the risk out of farming, or the industrial worker is told that most of their profits will go to the worker, or that the businessman is duped into the idea that socialism will arrange the economy so competition is limited; all these ideas appealed to the government to make these things all happen.

In the article ***The Spectrum of the Constitution Eagle*** I shared how I was first attracted to the Democratic Party. I was young and actually believed that the government should take care of us. Then when I saw how some of John F. Kennedy's policies began to destroy young people's motivation to work hard, be self-sufficient, take responsibility for one's own self, etc., I began to question these liberal ideas.

So, I became what I call a political isolationist. In time I was embracing the ideas of the republican philosophy and became a card-carrying republican. Now that I see that there is no difference between the democrats and republicans these days I am stepping back to be the political isolationist once again. It's my right to do so, however the way I see the federal government is moving it won't be long before the government will tell us how to vote.

Who's that guy in Venezuela? Chavez? —he'd really love us and may want to move over here. Not good.

Not good—not good in the direction we are moving.

SOMEONE IS FOOLING WITH THE SOUL OF AMERICA

October 15, 2009

In the news lately, we have learned that there is an aggressive movement to take the Ten Commandments from our rotundas. It is a sad to realize that our nation is steering its course toward a shameful crumple. There was a time when America was great because it was good; now, as Alexis de Tocqueville warned, we will cease to be great because decency is definitely fading from our lives. Someone is precariously fooling with the soul of America.

The very first commandment states: "Thou shalt have no other gods before me." For this cause our country was founded upon the principles of Christianity. We see the faith of our fathers written all through the history of this great nation. If we research meaningfully into our history we would soon recognize that the Architect of the universe had an impressive role in the birth of this nation. All of the "thou shalt not's" are embedded in our American values and laws. We need to be reminded about them with every opportunity and occasion, whether it is in public places or in our hearts.

Here, in America, the Founders guaranteed us freedom of religion—this means that we could worship whomever or whatever our souls desire. The reason they debated about separating church and state was that they did not want any one religious denomination to dictate what King Henry VIII, who had all these wives, of England did. It was against the Catholic Church's doctrine for one to divorce his wife, much less even marry again. However, when King Henry's wife was unable to bear him a son, the only way he could change the doctrine was to dissociate himself from the church; as a result he produced the Church of England.

This issue of separation of church and state was inserted by the Founders for a purpose: that religious conviction should, indeed, play an important part in our lives. And so when these atheists can cogitate that religion is unconstitutional they are so far off base by sightlessness and narrow vision. Even though, as Tocqueville noted that religion plays no direct role in the affairs of government, he realized that it had to be the most important institution governing the moral lives of the population of America. When he visited America he saw that the American people were worshipping in Christian churches

Just as other nations of the world embrace their own religious convictions, like the Muslims worship Allah; there are the Mohammed worshippers and then the people from the eastern and central orient believe in the teachings of Gautama Buddha. Native Americans appealed for guidance from the Great Spirit in the sky. Some of their earliest stories tell about this impressive white prophet who visited them for a short while and promised he would return to them one day. There is this book called He Walked the Americas by L. Taylor Hanson. It tells Native American stories and legends from South and North America about this person who came and tarried among them for some time teaching the people those same things that the Christian Prophet taught across the "land of many waters." This book is a clear account of a people who were taught Christianity long before Columbus discovered us. When the missionaries influenced the Indian nations with the bible, they were surprised that Native American stories and legends were similar to the accounts in the bible.

Our country was founded upon the principles of Christianity; it is written all through the history of this illustrious nation; the commandments are even embedded in our Native American values. The Battle Song of the Alaska Native Brotherhood is Onward Christian

Soldiers; when we take the oath of membership, or an office, in this organization we promise that we will look to our Heavenly Father for wisdom and strength to keep us steadfast. In times of war or disaster Americans, true Americans, does exactly that. And, indeed, we are strengthened.

All peoples of the world call for faith-based principles to rely on for their existence. We are no different, so why are these faithless based people in lofty places using their prominent positions by appeals from a few atheists to take away the foundation that made the people of America morally upright?

SOMETHING VERY REFRESHING

The Constitution of the United States

"A primary object ...should be the education of our youth in the science of government. In a republic, what species of knowledge can be equally important? And what duty more pressing than communicating it to those who are to be the future guardians of the liberties of the country."

—George Washington

One spring day I made an emergency trip to Juneau to have a broken front tooth repaired. I called my youngest son, Robert's home and talked to his wife, Victoria. I could hear the chatter of their children in the back ground. I told her that I was coming there to see the dentist. Without hesitation she insisted that I stay with them. "My sister and her two children from Utah are visiting," she said. "We'll be crowded here but I come from a large family and I love company," she added.

Robert met me at the airport. Upon arriving at their home, I was introduced to a small part of Victoria's extended family— her sister, Susan, Susan's thirteen-year-old daughter, Elisa, and a baby who was just beginning to walk.

They had already had dinner, so they sat me down and shoved a plat filled with food before me. At the same time Elisa had brought her lap top computer to the table and began to connect it. I learned that she is being home schooled and one of her courses of study was the U.S. Constitution—which is an online course from the National Center for Constitutional Studies. My interest perked up because I consider myself to be a constitution buff. Victoria knows this too and said "Grandpa can help you if you need it. He loves the Constitution."

Elisa had been working on her assignments and was doing only the questions that she knew with the intent of doing the harder ones later. Later was now and she gladly accepted my offer to mentor her.

I learned that Elisa was taking this course along with other students who were being home schooled. She said they meet often and discussed among themselves problems and share thoughts and observations.

I was reminded about when Alexis Tocqueville came to America to learn about our republic. One of the things he found was that in the homes and schools throughout the country the children were studying the Constitution—dissecting it, analyzing it and putting it back together. The purpose for doing so was to learn what the Founder's intent was for the American government so that if they ever had to defend our republic they would do it by common sense words rather than with the sword. When he returned home to France he wrote a book (1835 and 1840) called *Democracy in America*. In it he penned how America still embraced core values from the Founding Fathers. Three of those values were love of God, family, and country.

I think it is a sad day in our history when these basic values are no longer a part of our everyday living. Tocqueville describes the importance of the family unit. In those days, of course, families in America were very close. This was still true when I was growing up in this small rural community of Yakutat, Alaska. In grade school we sang "God Bless America," pledged allegiance to the flag and I began to take pride that we were very special people. In high school we had to recite the Preamble of the Constitution by heart. In contrast today we have a minister of the faith who wants God to "damn America."

In those days, and in ours, children were taught the value of work and loyalty to God, family and country; parents relied on the clergy to feed their spirits while hard work in the field provided rations to feed their bodies. Schools not only taught the 3R's but implanted in children's souls a principle upon which this country was founded upon: that of abiding by the Natural Laws. The first paragraph of the Declaration of Independence mentions the Laws of Nature and Nature's God—meaning that we should be entitled to have the blessings of nature and God. I'm thankful that I lived in a time when God, Family, Country really meant something. I am distressed that today the schools don't have in their curriculum anything about the true history of this country.

The Declaration of Independence addressed reasons why the colonists broke away from the mother country and why this particular government was created: to protect our lives, our liberties and pursuits of happiness. It also states in a following paragraph that when the governments no longer does these—that is the protection of our lives, our liberties and guarantees our pursuit of happiness, then it is the right of people to either alder or abolish it and start a new one based on those same principles—that is the protection of our lives, liberties and our pursuit of happiness. Now this might be a pretty radical statement, but when radical things are imposed upon us by the government, then we may have to use radical remedies.

One of the questions Elisa wondered about was the meaning of the Tenth Amendment to the Constitution. We talked about how the people delegated to the government to do certain things and that whatever is not empowered to the federal government is reserved for the state and/or to the people. There is also a provision in the Declaration that expresses where no law shall be made without the "consent of the governed." It was a thrill to see her eyes and face light up. "Oh, I see," she said, and would write her own thoughts about the subject. There were other parts in certain clauses that she asked about and the same reaction was revealed in her continence when clarity was revealed.

For a thirteen-year-old, I was impressed with her ability to grasp an idea, analyze and draw conclusions. I said to myself that if her group of young people is studying the Constitution, and there are others like them around the country, what a tribute it would be when they rise to the occasion to defend our lives, our liberties and our pursuit of happiness when our country is in dire danger of going astray. I have to say that I was very refreshed with this experience and am still bolstered when I think about it, which has been quite often of late. With these kinds of young people amongst us, there is hope for our republic.

May the Good Lord bless these young people, and may the Creator continue to bless America.

EPILOGUE

Following is a speech I gave at an Alaska Intertribal Council convention in Anchorage Alaska several years ago. It sums up everything that I have written in this volume.

Reclaiming our Power
We need Balance and both Feet on the Ground

Andrew P. Johnson was a Tlingit elder and educator who taught at Mt. Edgecumbe High School, a boarding school for Alaska Natives, and later at Sheldon Jackson College in Sitka Alaska. Not only was he able to achieve the credentials to teach in high school and college but he had a vast knowledge of Tlingit history, traditions and culture. This is what we call today, in the true sense of the phrase, traditional and ecological knowledge. I had the privilege of hearing him speak on occasion and always thought that if one could take Native American knowledge and bridge it with American values, what a powerful group of combined people we could be. While at Mt. Edgecumbe one of the courses Mr. Johnson taught was weight lifting. I never took any of his classes, but had friends who did, and one of the first principles they learned from him in lifting weights was this: "In order to do the bar bells correctly, you have to have good balance and both feet on the ground." What a timeless statement—even more so for this day and age for us as a human race. Over the many years I have spent trying to learn everything about everything I have understand that Tlingit people, and Native Americans in general, actually believe in balance. This is reflective in our society by marriage arrangements, clan structure and even in how they managed their resources.

I think we can all agree that there is a myriad of laws that affect our lives every day. To some of us there's God's laws that we hold onto for dear life, man's laws which translates to the laws of the federal, state, local governments that we are bonded by to try and use to guide our everyday affairs; there's Newton's law, mom and dad's laws—we can go on and on here…. But these laws are supposed to provide balance in our lives so that we can have the freedom to live in the ways we want to live that would enable us to pursue happiness.

Do we sometimes wonder where some of these laws come from? Where is their origin or source? How do we know which ones are proper for us? How can we tell if they will be detrimental to our health and wellbeing?

I think we can agree, also, that there are fundamental laws we all must learn to abide by. I believe if we want to succeed in life, it would be helpful to know and understand these laws so they can be utilized for our benefit.

When I was in college I took American Indian Education 101. It was in this classroom setting that I learned how Native Americans provided balance in their lives. In our first day of class our professor, who was Native American, drew a circle on the chalk board. In the circle he wrote the word NATURE. Outside of the circle he drew arrows that pointed to the lines of the circle. He explained that we, as Native people, used to live within that circle. "We lived with Nature," he said. "That is why our ancestors were in harmony with Nature. They were a part of Nature. They lived according to the Natural laws, and because they obeyed the natural laws Nature provided for us all that we needed." He explained that the arrows represented the outside influences that were to eventually come. They existed on the outside of the circle; their purpose was to inter in and conquer, and when they eventually did it caused this tremendous culture clash, this turmoil, this lack of balance, this usurpation and oppression into our lives. This is the clash of cultures that we as Native Americans are struggling to recover from to this day.

Now for the past two hundred years or more, the policies of the federal government were countless—from assimilation to extermination to termination to Indian reorganization, then to self-determination and self-governance. I think that self-governance has given us some hope, but now that was threatened by the reversal of the 9th Circuit Court of Appeals decision on Venetie; there's the State of Alaska's refusal to acknowledge tribal governments in Alaska; and on top of these there's Congresses' attempt to relinquishing our right to govern ourselves.

Perhaps it would be well to our advantage if we examined a few insights about some principles that will help us bring sanity and correctness, not only in our own lives, but in other lives as well.

Someone once said, "When you learn correct principles we learn to govern ourselves." What I would like to offer here is hope—hope that we can be a happy, freedom loving, and prosperous people again; and in the process of re-discovering these we may be able to help other people as well. There is a lot that our brothers and sisters throughout the world can learn from Native American and Alaska Native values.

I would like to start by sharing some principles given by the Founding Fathers from the grandfather of all Native organizations: the Alaska Native Brotherhood. I used to write a column for the Juneau Empire called *Kadashan's Corner*. Many from Southeast Alaska may have read them, and if you'll remember some of the first ones were about the Alaska Native Brotherhood and how I felt about this organization.

Kadashan Speaks: The Law of Nature and Nature's God

What's so impressive about the Alaska Native Brotherhood is that it has a solid constitution. This device has witnessed the challenges of the times; people have tried to amend it and replace it with great difficulty; men and women of rational minds have seen fit to respect the reflection, the anticipation and vision of its founding fathers so that we can still use these as a guide today.

There are timeless principles contained in the First Article of the Constitution. Here is how the Article reads:

> *The purpose of this organization shall be to assist and encourage the Native in his advancement from his native state to his place among the civilized races of the world; to oppose, to discourage, and to overcome the narrow injustice of race prejudice; to commemorate the fine qualities of the Native races of North America; to preserve their history, lore, art and virtues; to cultivate the morality, education, commerce, and civil government of Alaska; to improve individual and municipal health and laboring conditions, and to create a true respect in Natives and in other persons with whom they deal for the letter and spirit of the Declaration of Independence and the Constitution and laws of the United States.*

One thing in the first part of this article has bothered many Natives. It is in reference to advancing ourselves from our *Native state to be among the cultivated races of the world*. If we were to take the circle idea I shared with you earlier, this should be read the other way around. We all have to return back the principles of the *Natural Laws;* and then the other things would fall into place mentioned after that, such as opposing and discouraging race prejudice, preserving our history, etc. However, notwithstanding the other issues mentioned the things that stands out to me are those of cultivating the civil government of Alaska and that of creating a true respect in Natives and people with whom they deal under the *"spirit of the Declaration of Independence and the Constitution and laws of the United States."*

Which now follows other issues worthy to address: they are some principles contained in the Declaration of Independence; however, there is a definition of a word that is worth elaborating on for a second? It is this word *principle*. Webster says that it means a "general or fundamental law or doctrine; a rule or code of conduct; the laws or facts of nature; a primary source or origin." Therefore, we can conclude that a principle is something that is based upon the *natural law*. Our people had balance in their lives because they had learned by trial and error to abide by these inherent laws.

Let's examine a couple of principles in the Declaration. It states that all men are created equal in the eyes of the Creator. This may be easy to accept, but where we run into problems are when we must deal with this equality business between ourselves—other ethnic groups—other nationalities, etc. As I studied this over the past twenty years, I have come to the realization that we are not equal economically, socially, or politically. I think what the founding Fathers meant was that we all have the same equal opportunities, and it is up to us as individuals, as families, as villages and communities, and as a Native group to take advantage of those opportunities and advance ourselves economically, socially and politically. But the mechanisms must be there for us to make these happen. The early leaders of the Alaska Native Brotherhood and Sisterhood understood this and followed the principles that made them a great people under their own codes of conduct—principles that aided them in this task of survival for thousands of years. The one thing they had difficulty balancing was this equality issue, however they had leaders such as Elizabeth Peratrovich and her husband Roy who paved the way for equality.

Another thing the Declaration says is that we are all endowed with certain unalienable rights, and that these rights are the rights to the protection of our lives, our liberties, and the guarantee of our pursuit of happiness.

Let's elaborate on this word *unalienable* for a second. It is closely related to the word *principle* only it has to do with our rights. One definition is that it is a natural right. In other words, it's a right that comes from Nature. Another definition is that it is a "God given right." Whether it is a natural right or a God-given right, an unalienable right is a right that cannot be taken away. Therefore, no government, or department of government, has the power to take these away from us. Included in these rights are the right to govern ourselves and the taking and using of our traditional foods to sustain our lives, both temporally and spiritually. Instead of restricting use of these resources, governments should be protecting and guaranteeing these rights to us. That's the challenge that we, as tribal leaders representing our tribal governments, have today. We need to be free to chart our own destinies, to determine our prosperities, to bring happiness in our lives, our communities, etc.

Let's dwell a little here on the "pursuit of happiness" phrase. We are all in search of some kind of happiness—aren't we? I think that is the ultimate goal of all humankind. If we want to be a happy people there are certain basic needs that we have to take care of: food, shelter, clothing—. For example, in today's culture anyways, in order for us to take care of these needs we must own a business or work for someone who owns a business. If we want to start a business we have to have the right to own property, or if we work for someone else, that person must have the freedom to own property. If we want to sustain our families through a subsistence lifestyle, hunting, fishing or gathering, these are rights that should be guaranteed. We should also have the right to govern, and manage, these resources as well.

The Declaration of Independence states that the purpose for forming the government was to protect our lives, our liberties, and to guarantee our pursuit of happiness—that anything more or less than these are either usurpation or oppression, and when our government(s) no longer does these things—that is protect our lives, liberties and guarantee us happiness, then it is up to the American people to alter or abolish that government and start a new one based on those same principles—that is the protection of our lives, our liberties, and our pursuit of happiness.

Kadashan Speaks: The Law of Nature and Nature's God

Now I don't believe we are at a point where we have to abolish our government just yet, but we surely can do a lot of altering.

Now, we all know who the founding Fathers of this nation were; they have been imbedded in our hearts and minds since grade school. A few of the main ones immediately comes to mind: Jefferson, Madison, Washington, Franklin, and Adams. These men were ably educated about the things of the world of their time; they were ably versed in history, economics, political science, philosophy, literature and other sciences. Having studied the history of nations that have come and gone, they understood why greatness was achieved and why grandeur faded.

It's interesting to note that all great nations that have come and gone were never conquered from without—they fell because of erosion from within. Is there a lesson to be learned here? Well, anyway, the founders understood the successes and failures of other countries, and having some bad experiences with their mother country, they took these lessons of history and their experiences and painstakingly formulated an instrument that would be an ensign to the world.

And included in the incorporation of this document were the principles of the Great Bind Law of the Iroquois, the Confederate Tribes, or the so-called Six Civilized Tribes. Adams, Jefferson, Franklin, Madison, and others, came to know and understand these people and their ways. They visited their villages and learned their culture—even learned the languages. These tribes had a very sophisticated government. It is from this confederacy that the Founding Fathers learned about state's rights, representative form of government, and women suffrage. It is from these tribes that they also learned an important concept: control comes from the bottom and works its way up instead of from the top down as it is practiced today.

When I was in college I took a course in the U.S. Constitution. As we studied its background and origin I learned why America became the fastest growing and most powerful nation the world has ever known. No other nation has come close to achieving what it was able to do. In less than 50 years it began to flex its muscles that caused other nations throughout the world to sit up and immediately take notice.

As I studied and pondered and prayed about these issues, I realized that the only way we could become a strong, freedom loving people again was to go back to the true —the original—intent of the principles contained in the United States Constitution and to bring back the values that Native American and Alaska Natives embraced in their lives that are no longer with us. Living the Law of Nature and Nature's God include principles that can make America great once again.

When I attended my first Self-Governance Conference in 1993 and started rubbing elbows with powerful tribal leaders like the Joe Dela Cruze's, the Ron Allen's, the Henry Cagey's, Danny Jordan's, G.I James, and many other tribal leaders across the country, who were the movers and shakers of the Self-Governance Demonstration Project, I sat and listened for about a half a day. When we had a break I went to my room and fell to my knees and thanked the Creator for what I had been learning. I was finding answers to many questions I had been asking and searching and pondering upon for nearly my entire lifetime.

What we are doing here with self-governance for Native Americans and Alaska Natives is noble. Let us stay on this course. And while we are doing the right thing, let us do the right thing right for the right purposes; in so doing we must base these right things on correct principles. Might come from right, not the reverse. I think the lashing challenge we have in these trying times is to go back to principles that works in a positive way for us.

We don't need a reformation of anything. What we need is a restoration of old values. When we learn correct principles we will learn to govern ourselves; we will become balanced with both feet on the ground. If we truly want this to happen we will have to go back to abiding by the *Natural Law* of success. And in the process of doing, searching, finding, re-discovering, restoring and reclaiming our power, perhaps we can help America come back on the right track as well.

That is what I would like this book to accomplish. I believe we can.

BIBLIOGRAPHY

1. Wampum Belts and Peace Trees, Gregory Schaaf, 1990, Fulcrum Printing

2. The Living U. S. Constitution_ *Saul K Pad over,* 1953, *Mentor Books*

3. The 5000 Year Leap, W. Cleon Skousen, copyright 2012 by C& J Investments

4. The Making of America, The Substance and Meaning of the Constitution, W. Cleon Skousen, copyright 1985

5. Action for Americans, The Liberty Amendment, Lloyd G. Herbarreith and Gordon van B. King, 1963, Operation of America

6. An Enemy Hath Done This, Ezra Taft Benson, 1969, Parliament Publishers, Inc. 5. This Nation Shall Stand, Ezra Taft Benson, 1977, Deseret Book Company

7. The American Indian—Prehistory to the Present, *Arell Morgan Gibson 1980, D. C. Heath and Company*

8. Great Speeches *by* Native Americans, Dover Publication, 2000

9. American Indian Myths and Legends, 1984, by Richard Erdoes and Alfonso Ortiz

10. Indian Self Rule 1986 Howe Brothers

11. The Native Brotherhoods: Modem Intertribal Organizations on the Northwest Coast, 1958, Smithsonian Institution Bureau of American Ethnology, Bulletin 168

12. The Federalist Papers, Hamilton, Madison, Jay, 1961, Mentor Books

13. Alaska Natives Commission Final Report, Volume I

14. Democracy in America, New Rochelle, New York, Arlington House

15. Works, Thomas Jefferson

16. Our Oriental Heritage, Will Durant, Simon and Schuster, 1954

17. Under Mount Saint Elias, The History and Culture of the Yakutat Tlingit, Frederica de Laguna

www.ingramcontent.com/pod-product-compliance
Lightning Source LLC
Chambersburg PA
CBHW031147020426
42333CB00013B/542